This journal belongs to

Jane E. Millward

(Gift from Martha Holley, early 2000's)

You are a beloved child of God,

precious to Him in every way. As you seek Him, He will show you
the mysteries of life and unfold His unique plans for you—
a life full of rich blessing.

God cares about you and knows all the desires of your heart.
He is as close as breathing. Let this journal inspire you to express
your thoughts, record your prayers, embrace your dreams,
and listen to what God is saying to you.

Be strong in the Lord, and may His presence guide your heart always.

The LORD your God is with you…. He will quiet you with his love.

ZEPHANIAH 3:17 NIV

BE STILL
AND KNOW
that I am God

PROMISE JOURNAL

...inspired by life

Be Still and Know

Bestow upon me, O Lord my God, understanding to know Thee,
diligence to seek Thee, wisdom to find Thee, and a faithfulness
that may finally embrace Thee.

THOMAS AQUINAS

Perhaps this moment is unclear, but let it be—even if the next,
and many moments after that are unclear, let them be.
Trust that God will help you work them out, and that all the unclear
moments will bring you to that moment of clarity and action
when you are known by Him and know Him.
These are the better and brighter moments of His blessing.

WENDY MOORE

We must concentrate on knowing God; the more we know Him
the more we want to know Him. And as knowledge is commonly
the measure of love, the deeper and wider our knowledge,
the greater will be our love.

BROTHER LAWRENCE

They who seek the throne of grace
Find that throne in every place;
If we live a life of prayer,
God is present everywhere.

OLIVER HOLDEN

Monday, August 8, 2022

> Isaiah 1:16-17; the topic of Bob Clark's
  "Encouragement" radio spot during Point of
  View radio talk show - WLPE 91.7 FM
> (P.O.V. r.t.s. - 1st hr., _Eight House_, Tevvy Troy;
  2nd hr., H. Sterling Burnett, Heartland Institute,
  exposé re: global warming)

Tues., 8-09-22
> Hymn: How Gentle God's Commands (P. Doddridge)

Wed., 8-10-22
> _Valley of Vision_:
   God the Spirit, p. 52; Caring Love, p. 210;
   Grace Active, p. 214
> Mason's _Gospel ATJ_, pp. 133-4: Job 11:7-8 (control)
> Psalm 119: 73-80; Pss. 59; 56; 94

*B*e still, and know that I am God!

PSALM 46:10 NLT

Audience of One

Solitude liberates us from entanglements by carving out a space
from which we can see ourselves and our situation before
the Audience of One. Solitude provides the private place where we can
take our bearings and so make God our North Star.

OS GUINNESS

Solitude begins with a time and place for God, and God alone.
If we really believe not only that God exists but also that He
is actively present in our lives—healing, teaching, guiding—we need to
set aside a time and space to give Him our undivided attention.

HENRI J. M. NOUWEN

When you pray, go away by yourself, shut the door behind you,
and pray to your Father in private. Then your Father,
who sees everything, will reward you.

MATTHEW 6:6 NLT

You have set Your glory above the heavens.
Thy glory flames from sun and star:
Center and soul of every sphere,
yet to each loving heart how near.

OLIVER WENDELL HOLMES

Thurs., 8-11-22

> Hymns : 113 - My Soul with Expectation
(Ps.62); 331- Lead Kindly Light (Nos.
from ~~the Hymnbook~~*); also 114- I Look to
Thee in Every Need (Samuel Longfellow, 1864)

  *Copyright, MCMLV, BY John Ribble (Eighteenth Printing)

viewpoints.info/crt

> Recent commentaries (view points) by Kerby Anderson :

  8-10-22 : Foresees the demise of all but the
  prestigious universities as brick & mortar
  facilities; others will tend toward online learning alone

  8-11-22 : Shares Dennis Prager's thoughts about
  what makes America unique vs. Europe
  following (since) WWI — patriotism and Judeo-Christian
  ethic; Russia went with Communism, Italy
  with Facism, Germany with Nazism

        - - - - -

New Pacific Garden Mission offerings :
  1) The Clue Crew
  2) History's Greatest Sermons
  3) Daily Devotional (3 mins.)

This announcement heard 7-17-22; WLPE, 91.7 FM.
  Already heard on WLPE and WYFA (BBN, 107.1 FM):
  (aired)   PGM's "Unshackled" 30-min. program.

When we focus on God, the scene changes. He's in control of our lives;
nothing lies outside the realm of His redemptive grace.

PENELOPE J. STOKES

Sharing with God

Prayer is such an ordinary, everyday, mundane thing. Certainly, people who pray are no more saints than the rest of us. Rather, they are people who want to share a life with God, to love and be loved, to speak and to listen, to work and to be at rest in the presence of God.

ROBERTA BONDI

God still draws near to us in the ordinary, commonplace, everyday experiences and places.... He comes in surprising ways.

HENRY GARIEPY

There is an essential connection between experiencing God, loving God, and trusting God. You will trust God only as much as you love Him, and you will love Him to the extent you have touched Him, rather that He has touched you.

BRENNAN MANNING

The impetus of God's love comes from within Himself, to share with us His life and love. It is a beautiful, eternal gift, held out to us in the hands of love. All we have to do is say "Yes!"

JOHN POWELL

Sunday, 8-14-22

> Romans 4:18; Hebrews 11:27c
  Jeremiah 43:6; 41:10; 38:23 - "king's daughters,"
  "princesses" - why specified (chs. 41, 43)? (Ch. 38, v.
  23 cross-ref. to 41:10 in ESV.)

> Hymn: "Hail to the Lord's Anointed"

Thurs., 8-25-22

Hymns, early A.M.

> The Lord is never far away, but through all
  grief distressing, an ever-present
  help and stay. To God all praise
  and glory. (Hymn title?) Be joyful in
  the Lord, my soul, Both soul and body bear
  your part.

> the Lord's My Shepherd, I'll Not Want

> God, the Omnipotent (Russian Hymn) - 461 in
  Worship and Service Hymnal

> Daily Bread reading (R. M. M'Cheyne)
  I Sam. 17:26b, 32a, 34-36 ["used to keep" - David
  had a plan (or goal) in mind, in reliance on
  God & for his glory] / forty days Israeli army was
                          taunted; forty days Jesus spent
                          in the wilderness

I'll lead you to buried treasures, secret caches of valuables—
Confirmations that it is, in fact, I, GOD...who calls you by your name.

ISAIAH 45:3 MSG

The Best Times

When you open up the Bible and you pray the Scriptures back to God,
you're experiencing something really wonderful.... He's delighted.
The silence confirms that we are His people. We are talking
and God is listening. But the best times are when God starts talking,
and we're quiet enough to hear Him.

CALVIN MILLER

That is God's call to us—simply to be people who are content
to live close to Him and to renew the kind of life in which
the closeness is felt and experienced.

THOMAS MERTON

I have set the LORD always before me....
Therefore my heart is glad and my tongue rejoices;
my body also will rest secure....
You have made known to me the path of life;
you will fill me with joy in your presence,
with eternal pleasures at your right hand.

PSALM 16:8–9, 11 NIV

The kiss of eternal life, and the warm embrace of God's Word,
are so sweet, and bring such pleasure, that you can never
become bored with them; you always want more.

HILDEGARD OF BINGEN

8-25-22 (Thurs.)

> Daily Bible Reading (M'Cheyne)

Romans 15:1-7, 16b, 29

8-26-22 (Friday)

> Hymn: O God, the Rock of Ages (based on Ps. 90) –

Bickersteth / Holbrook ; Tune, MIRIAM : 7.6.7.6.D;

92 in The Hymnbook (Copyright MCMLV (1955) by John

Ribble, 18th printing; Publishing Agent, THE

HYMNBOOK, 929 Witherspoon Building, Philadelphia 7,

Pennsylvania)

Sat., 8-27-22

> The Public Square

- Modeled their techniques on the radio
  show "A Prairie Home Companion"

- Highly recommend using the "Blue Letter
  Bible" website for free access to bible study
  resources; illustrated using Prov. 15:5 (NIV)
  and the word sometimes translated as <u>father</u>,
  other times as <u>parent</u>. "Words matter." (D.2.)

- Avail. fr. P.Sq. – <u>His Story</u> (chronological life
  of Jesus fr. the four gospels)

- Discussion of Maralago press releases; e.g. <u>Washington Post</u>

*I*t is God's love for us that He not only gives us His Word
but also lends us His ear.

DIETRICH BONHOEFFER

Blessed Assurance

So wait before the Lord; Wait in the stillness. And in that stillness,
assurance will come to you. You will know that you are heard;
you will know that your Lord ponders the voice
of your humble desires; you will hear quiet words
spoken to you yourself, perhaps to your grateful surprise
and refreshment.

AMY CARMICHAEL

In those times I can't seem to find God,
I rest in the assurance He knows how to find me.

NEVA COYLE

Peace *with* God brings the peace *of* God. It is a peace
that settles our nerves, fills our mind, floods our spirit,
and in the midst of the uproar around us, gives us
the assurance that everything is all right.

BOB MUMFORD

Do not be anxious about anything, but in everything,
by prayer and petition, with thanksgiving, present your requests to God.
And the peace of God, which transcends all understanding,
will guard your hearts and your minds in Christ Jesus.

PHILIPPIANS 4:6–7 NIV

Sat., 8-27-22 (Late P.M.)
> Wm. MacDonald's One Day At A Time, Aug. 28—
    Numbers 32:23 ; p. 252 ; poem: "The Dream of Eugene Aram"
> Hymn : Jesus Only, Let Me See, by Oswald J. Smith
    (Music : Daniel B. Towner ; 344 in Worship and Service
    Hymnal)
Sunday, 8-28-22
> Hymn : There's a Wideness in God's Mercy
> Daily Light, Bagster/Lotz (Rev. 12:10 et. al. plus
                                        1 John 4:18)
> Faith's Checkbook, Spurgeon (Ps. 55:16 ; Look to God for
    Hymn : If thou But Suffer   help in troubling circumstances—
              God to Guide Thee   to God only)

> Keep a Quiet Heart, Elisabeth Elliot ; Pp. 199-200 :
    "The Taking of Human Life," with two contrasting
    examples, one of Texas inmate's death by
    lethal injection, the other of a twin fetus
    being aborted by needle "abortion" in utero.*
    Romans 12:1-2 referenced about thinking
    Christianly vs. worldly thought ; need to believe,
    hear, and obey.
    *With marked difference in public interest for detailed info.
      Example taken from Times Magazine article, Dec. 20, 1982
    and earlier news story (source unidentified ; a few mos. earlier)

*Be assured, if you walk with Him and look to Him
and expect help from Him, He will never fail you.*

GEORGE MUELLER

Fill Me Up, Lord

When I am in solitude, the presence of God is so real and so full
that there is nothing else I want. The people I love are with me
in God's presence, beyond the surface choppiness of all the stresses
that separate us as finite beings on this earth, and I am able
to experience our ultimate togetherness in God. This experience
is absolutely the only thing that fills the longing of my heart.

RUTH HALEY BARTON

The LORD will guide you always;
he will satisfy your needs in a sun-scorched land
and will strengthen your frame.
You will be like a well-watered garden,
like a spring whose waters never fail.

ISAIAH 58:11 NIV

Prayer is to the spirit what breath is to the body.
We treat prayer as though it were the spice of life,
but the Bible prescribes it as a vital staple in our diet.

DAVID HUBBARD

Solitude is for those with an ample interior, with room to roam,
well-provided with supplies. And I need a day or two,
every so often, to make the journey.

CATHERINE CALVERT

Sunday, 8-28-22
> Two wedding hymns, <u>Worship and Service Hymnal</u>:
   524 O perfect love, all human thought
             transcending (Dorothy Gurney / Joseph Barnby)
   525 A Wedding Prayer (Alfred P. Gibbs)
> Evening hymns - Topic: Joy (from <u>The Hymnal</u>)
   411 Take the Name of Jesus with You
   410 The King of Glory Standeth
Monday, 8-30-22
Hymn: Lead, Kindly Light (all 3 vss.)
Friday, 9-02-22
> 1 Cor. 7:36-38 (<u>ESV</u>): seems to say a couple
able to exercise self-control may remain in a
state of betrothal and forego marriage(?) - a
"permanently engagement"? Without cohabi-
tation, as a betrothed couple in bible times?
> On BBN's Conference Pulpit, Aug. 29-31 & Sept. 1,
2022 - Craig Massey preaching / teaching about
what a husband owes his wife (8/29-31) &
vice versa (9/01). The object is to have a home based
on motivation and love rather than manipulation
and intimidation (BBN announcer - H.F.? - follow-up
                            statement.)

*O*ur love to God arises out of our emptiness;
God's love to us out of His fullness.

HANNAH MORE

Only in Silence

If we really want to pray, we must first learn to listen:
for in the silence of the heart, God speaks. And to be able to see
that silence, to be able to hear God, we need a clean heart.
Let us listen to God, to what He has to say. We cannot speak
unless we have listened, unless we have made our connection with God.

MOTHER TERESA

It is in silence that God is known,
and through mysteries that He declares Himself.

ROBERT H. BENSON

I wait quietly before God,
for my victory comes from him....
Let all that I am wait quietly before God,
for my hope is in him.

PSALM 62:1, 5 NLT

If Jesus Christ is bringing you into the understanding
that prayer is for the glorifying of His Father,
then He will give you the first sign of His intimacy—silence.

OSWALD CHAMBERS

There is a silence into which the world cannot intrude.
There is a peace you carry in your heart and cannot lose.

Friday, Sept. 2, 2022

"Christianity is valuable only if it is personal."
— A. Korbel (from autobiography of her
husband, Joseph Korbel, on Moody Radio's
Stories of Great Christians: <u>In My Enemy's
Camp</u>, aired Aug. /Sept. 2022 on BBN radio)
Ch. 26; Sept. 2, 2022 air date

Sat., 9-03-22

> <u>Voices of the Saints</u>, Bert Ghezzi:
144 Gregory the Great (540? -604)
145 Gregory the Wonderworker (213? -270?)
214 Kentigern (518? -603)
76 Columba (521? - 597)
105 Faustina Kowalska (1905 -1938)
140 Gregory Lopez (1542 -1596)

> 1 Cor. 8:6   One God, the Father; one Lord, Jesus Christ

Ezekiel 6:9   God's heart broken

Ps. 44:20b / vv. 20-21; cf. Job 11:13 (ESV) / Rev. 3:1-6   seven spirits of God; seven stars; dressed in white

> <u>The Gospel According to Job</u>, Mike Mason
Job 11:14-15; Cheap Guilt, pp. 135-6; incl.
Oswald Chambers quote about worship

*We receive only when we are recollected; only in silence
is heard the beating of the heart of God.*

FATHER BERNARDO OLIVERA

The Desire to Know

In extravagance of soul we seek His face. In generosity of heart,
we glean His gentle touch. In excessiveness of spirit,
we love Him and His love comes back to us a hundredfold.

TRICIA MCCARY RHODES

Late have I loved You,
O beauty so ancient and so new.
Late have I loved You!
You were within me while I
have gone outside to seek You.
Unlovely myself, I rushed towards
all those lovely things You had made.
And always You were with me.

AUGUSTINE

If we really want to know God, we will seek Him. As we start
to enjoy His divine companionship, experience His peace,
and trust His direction, we will crave more of Him
in every area of our lives. We will come to a place where He will
ask us what we want, and we will simply say, "You, Lord—
not your blessings, not what you can do for us—only You."

AMY AND JUDGE REINHOLD

Sat., 9-03-22

Voices of the Saints, B. Ghezzi

   97 Ephrem (306? – c. 373?): headmaster,
     hymnwriter; empathic

Sunday, 9-04-22

> Daily Light (Bagster, Lotz)/A.M. – Ruth 3:3 et. al.,
Isa. 30:15 & 28:16 included; quiet resting, listening to God,
believing him

> Hymns: Ask Ye What Great Thing I Know; Grace
and Truth Shall Mark the Way; Come, Ye
Disconsolate, Where'er Ye Languish (371, 2, 3
in The Hymnbook); Topic: Faith and assurance;
373, v. 3 also references Lord's Supper; all three
verses ref. heaven

- Spirit of God, Descend Upon My Heart – v. 2 –
compare c̄ 1 Samuel 28 (also hymn, v.s. 3)

- I Know Whom I Have Believed

- I Know Not How That Bethlehem's Babe (224 in
The Hymnbook): three verses – Christ's life,
death, and resurrection

- I Know I Love Thee Better, Lord (Frances Havergal):
45 in Praise and Worship Hymnal (Kansas City, Missouri:
Final line of chorus references Lillenas Publshg. Co.)
     Christ's blood

Keep on asking, and you will receive what you ask for. Keep on seeking,
and you will find. Keep on knocking, and the door will be opened to you.

MATTHEW 7:7 NLT

→ 4th & final verse speaks of heaven / being in God's (Christ's) presence

A Centered Life

Life from the Center is a life of unhurried peace and power.
It is simple. It is serene...: We need not get frantic. He is at the helm.
And when our little day is done, we lie down quietly in peace,
for all is well.

THOMAS R. KELLY

Drop thy still dews of quietness
till all our strivings cease;
take from our souls the strain and stress,
and let our ordered lives confess
the beauty of Thy peace.

JOHN GREENLEAF WHITTIER

Because we are spiritual beings...it is for our good, individually
and collectively, to live our lives in interactive dependence upon God.

DALLAS WILLARD

There is nothing but God's grace. We walk upon it; we breathe it;
we live and die by it; it makes the nails and axles of the universe.

ROBERT LOUIS STEVENSON

For of Him and through Him and to Him are all things,
to whom be glory forever. Amen.

ROMANS 11:36 NKJV

Sunday, 9-04-22

> Hymn - I Know of a Name (a.k.a. That
Beautiful Name); 146 in _Crowning Glory
Hymnal_ (Grand Rapids, Michigan : Singspiration,
Inc.; Worldwide Distribution, Zondervan
Publishing House; 1964) / Christmas hymn;
words by Jean Perry, alt., music, Mabel
Johnston Camp

> _Morning and Evening_, Spurgeon - June 15,
morning - Genesis 21:6 - Sarah's Isaac,
(Mary's and) my Jesus - "Surprised by grace"
(Subject Index, p.751; Peabody, Massachusetts :
Hendrickson Publishers, Inc., 1991; ISBN 978-1-
59856-569-0). Also, I Samuel 2:1 - Hannah's
rejoicing over Samuel

Monday, 9-05-2022

> John Campbell Shairp poem, "the Sure Hold of God"
(June 26, 1988 FPC-Augusta, GA ~~frontispiece~~ bulletin)

> Hymn : Abide with Me : Fast Falls the Eventide
(Henry F. Lyte / William H. Monk.; 19th century)
See esp. v. 3 (5 vss. in _The Hymnbook_ - No. 64)
+ v. 2

ℱor in him we live and move and have our being.

ACTS 17:28 NIV

Rhythms and Patterns

In waiting we begin to get in touch with the rhythms of life—
stillness and action, listening and decision. They are the rhythms
of God. It is in the everyday and the commonplace
that we learn patience, acceptance, and contentment.

RICHARD J. FOSTER

Love comes while we rest against our Father's chest.
Joy comes when we catch the rhythms of His heart.
Peace comes when we live in harmony with those rhythms.

KEN GIRE

In the process of creation and relationship, what seems mundane
and trivial may show itself to be holy, precious, part of a pattern.

LUCI SHAW

It's in Christ that we find out who we are and what we are living for.
Long before we first heard of Christ and got our hopes up,
he had His eye on us, had designs on us for glorious living,
part of the overall purpose he is working out
in everything and everyone.

EPHESIANS 1:11–12 MSG

Get the pattern of your life from God,
then go about your work and be yourself.

PHILLIPS BROOKS

Monday, 9-05-22
BBN Conf. Pulpit - Stuart Latimer:
"Biblical Viewpoint of Work"
Choral piece c̄ nice harmony, about heaven:
"Beautiful home of the ransomed, beside
    the crystal sea"...   (also on BBN,
    right after Conf. Pulpit)

Tuesday, 9-6-2022
> Spurgeon's Morning, in Jim Reimann's
  Look Unto Me: The Devotions of Charles
  Spurgeon (Day 250) - ends with verse 1
  of Thomas Toke Lynch's "Gracious Spirit,
  Dwell With Me"; scriptures cited: Phil. 2:14-16;
  Acts 8: 26-39; 20:26 (Spurgeon); John 8:12; 9:5;
  3:19,21. Light guides, warns, cheers.   A Christian's job
                                            description
> Day 249 in Whispers of Friendship: Daily
  Encouragement for Women (Urichsville, Ohio:
  Barbour Publishing, Inc., 2009; compiled by
  Kathy Shutt; ISBN 978-1-61626-414-7) -
  D.L. Moody's "Love Is" - 8 character traits
                    describing what love is,
                    from Gal. 5:22-23a

 The patterns of our days are always changing...rearranging...
and each design for living is unique...graced with its own special beauty.

Prayer Is...

Prayer is the deliberate and persevering action of the soul. It is true
and enduring, and full of grace. Prayer fastens the soul to God
and makes it one with God's will, through the deep
inward working of the Holy Spirit.

JULIAN OF NORWICH

We pray not to get something, but to open up a two-way street
between us and God, so that we and others
may inwardly become something.

JOHN HEUSS

Prayer is neither chiefly begging for things, nor is it merely
self-communion; it is that loftiest experience
within the reach of any soul, communion with God.

HARRY EMERSON FOSDICK

Our Father in heaven,
Hallowed be Your name.
Your kingdom come.
Your will be done
On earth as it is in heaven.
Give us this day our daily bread.
And forgive us our debts,
As we forgive our debtors.
And do not lead us into temptation,
But deliver us from the evil one.
For Yours is the kingdom
and the power and the glory forever.
Amen.

MATTHEW 6:9–13 NKJV

Tuesday, 9-6-2022

> Psalm hymns : 143; 48 (When Morning Lights the Eastern Skies; Within thy Temple's Sacred Courts)

> The Light of the Psalms, Michael F. Ross (Ross-shire, Scotland : Christian Focus Publications, Ltd.: 2006; ISBN 978-1-84550-150-1, Pbk.; ISBN 1-84550-150-0, Hardcover) – Psalm 143 – Day 42 in Part One : God Our Refuge, pp.72-79; includes Rom. Cath. "Act of Contrition" prayer; considered related to David's experiencing Absolam's rebellion. Scripture cited : 1 John 5:3.

> the Message of Romans : An Exposition, Robert C. McQuilkin (Columbia, SC : Columbia Int'l. Univ., 2015; First printing :1947; ISBN-13: 978-1-939074-06-5) – Lesson 8: Triumphant Life in the Spirit, Romans 8:14-39; Page 97 speaks of it not being good for large numbers of church attendees, who may/may not be saved, to all pray the Lord's Prayer.

The possibilities of prayer run parallel with the promises of God. Prayer opens an outlet for the promises...and secures their precious ends.

E. M. BOUNDS

Wait on the Lord

God never abandons anyone on whom He has set His love;
nor does Christ, the good shepherd, ever lose track of His sheep.
How slow we are to believe in God as God, sovereign, all-seeing
and almighty! We need to "wait upon the Lord" in meditations
on His majesty, till we find our strength renewed
through the writing of these things upon our hearts.

J. I. PACKER

Those who wait on the LORD
Shall renew their strength;
They shall mount up with wings like eagles,
They shall run and not be weary,
They shall walk and not faint.

ISAIAH 40:31 NKJV

When I need a dose of wonder I wait for a clear night
and go look for the stars.... In the country the great river
of the Milky Way streams across the sky, and I know that our planet
is a small part of that river of stars.... Often the wonder of the stars
is enough to return me to God's loving grace.

MADELEINE L'ENGLE

Thursday, 9-08-2022   (Queen Eliz. II homegoing)

> Hymn: How Can I Be Lonely? (Four vss., 3rd
  on bereavement; words & music by Haldor
  Lillenas, Copyright 1928 by Lillenas Publishing Co. -
  Int'l. copyright secured; 155 in Praise and
  Worship Hymnal; Kansas City, Missouri:
  Lillenas Publishing Company)

> Hymn, D. L. Moody's favorite, pp. 80-81 in   *(19th century)
  Ray Stedman's Waiting for the Second Coming:
  Studies in Thessalonians (Grand Rapids,
  Michigan: Discovery House Publishers, 1990).
  Hymn title? Immanuel's Land?" ... glory,   Chorus: → (vss. 1+2)
  glory dwelleth In Immanuel's land;" "The lamb   → (vs. 3)
  is all the glory Of Immanuel's land." Also,

v.1 "The sands of time are sinking, The dawn of
    heaven breaks;" ...

v.2 "O Christ, He is the fountain, The deep, sweet
    well of love!" ...

v.3 "the Bride eyes not her garment,
    But her dear Bridegroom's face;" ...

    * (Words by Elizabeth Clephane, from Scottish Covenanter
       of 17th century persecution, Samuel Rutherford's letter)

You are a little less than angels, crown of creation, image of God.
Each person is a revelation, a transfiguration,
a waiting for Him to manifest himself.

EDWARD FARRELL

Approach the Throne

I don't know, when I'm asking for something here on earth,
what is going on in the innermost shrine of Heaven (I like to think
about it, though). I am sure of one thing: it is good. Because Jesus
is there. Jesus loves me. Jesus has gone into that shrine on my behalf.
The hope we have is a living hope, an unassailable one.
We wait for it, in faith and patience.

ELISABETH ELLIOT

If you keep this comparison always in mind—that of a castle
with a wondrous throne within—God may use it to draw you
into His presence, where He bestows the favors that He loves to grant.

TERESA OF AVILA

I lift up my eyes to the hills—
where does my help come from?
My help comes from the LORD,
the Maker of heaven and earth.

PSALM 121:1–2 NIV

God is always on duty in the temple of your heart, His home....
It is the place where Someone takes your trouble
and changes it into His treasure.

BARBARA JOHNSON

Friday, 9-09-22

> Pss. 40 & 51, plus hymns : I Waited for the
  Lord My God; God, Be Merciful to Me

> Hymns : Go, Labor On: Spend, and Be Spent;
  Draw Thou My Soul, O Christ

Sat., 9-10-22   (a.k.a. American Policy Roundtable)
> The Public Square (Sept. 1st) speech = continuation of
       Pres. Biden's (recent) speech   Obama's final speech
  Topic : Equality & Democracy - not in U.S.   ∧ when
                          Declaration of Independence,   Pres.,
  Constitution, ∧ Bill of Rights, any early docs.   per
                                                        Dave
  ┌──┐ Z.
  │ (800) 522-8638 - call for copy of Jesus'   │
  │ Story (or Jesus : His Story) - chronological   │
  │   or online order :   │
  │ compilation of the four gospels The Public Square.com │
  └──┘

> The Valley of Vision : Puritan Prayers and
  Devotions - The Throne, pp. 272-3;
  To Be Fit For God, pp. 254-5; In Prayer,
  pp. 264-5; Seventh Day Evening : Future
  Blessings, pp. 404-5

> Grace for the Moment, Vol. I, Max Lucado -
  Who Can Fathom Eternity? (Eccl. 3:10 TLB;
  1 Cor. 2:9 (NCV), from his book When God
  Whispers Your Name

I lift up mine eyes to the quiet hills, and my heart to the Father's throne;
in all my ways, to the end of days, the Lord will preserve His own.

TIMOTHY DUDLEY-SMITH

Our Gracious God

The grace of God means something like: Here is your life.
You might never have been, but you *are* because the party
wouldn't have been complete without you. Here is the world.
Beautiful and terrible things will happen. Don't be afraid.
I am with you. Nothing can ever separate us. It's for you
I created the universe. I love you.

FREDERICK BUECHNER

God makes everything come out right;
he puts victims back on their feet....
As high as heaven is over the earth,
so strong is his love to those who fear him.
And as far as sunrise is from sunset,
he has separated us from our sins.

PSALM 103:6, 11–12 MSG

His overflowing love delights to make us
partakers of the bounties He graciously imparts.

HANNAH MORE

The joyful birds prolong the strain,
their song with every spring renewed;
the air we breathe, and falling rain,
each softly whispers: God is good.

JOHN HAMPDEN GURNEY

Grace means that God already loves us
as much as an infinite God can possibly love.

PHILIP YANCEY

Wed., 9-14-22

> Point of View's 50-yr. gala, wk. of 9-26-22
P.O.V. supported by Jeremiah Johnston,
Christian Thinker's Society (~~spt~~ spot anncmnt.);
also John Stonestreet

> Kerby Anderson's brief "Point of View" topic:
medical school student applicant questions
being targeted at D.E.I. – diversity,
equity, and inclusion – not new to college
campuses. Why not just ask "Why do you
want to be a physician?"

Friday, 9-16-22 "...we are (always)
> 2 Cor. 5:6-8 -- "of good courage"; "at home... in /with
for
...away; "the body ... the Lord."

> 2 Cor. 5:17, 21; Psalm 65:3

> Hymns: Thy Might Sets Fast the Mountains (Ps. 65):
same tune as Stand Up, Stand Up for Jesus, and
The Morning Light Is Breaking – Webb /Geo. J.
Webb, 1837 – Nos. 99, 349, 499 in <u>The Hymnbook</u>; *
(Yesterday): We Praise Thee, O God, Our Redeemer –
No. 17 in <u>The Hymnbook</u> (Julia C. Cory); Old Netherlands
Melody
* ... our Redeemer, Creator...

Delight in the Lord

Trust in the LORD and do good;
dwell in the land and enjoy safe pasture.
Delight yourself in the LORD
and he will give you the desires of your heart.
Commit your way to the LORD;
trust in him and he will do this:
He will make your righteousness shine like the dawn,
the justice of your cause like the noonday sun.
Be still before the LORD and wait patiently for him.

PSALM 37:3–7 NIV

God's pursuit of praise from us and our pursuit of pleasure in Him
are one and the same pursuit. God's quest to be glorified and our quest
to be satisfied reach their goal in this one experience:
our delight in God which overflows in praise.

JOHN PIPER

I rejoice in following your statutes
as one rejoices in great riches.
I meditate on your precepts
and consider your ways.
I delight in your decrees;
I will not neglect your word.

PSALM 119:14–16 NIV

Sunday, 9-18-22
> Hymns: O Let My Supplicating Cry (Ps. 119);
New Every Morning Is The Love — both use
the tune Melcombe. See The Hymnbook —
Nos. 323 and 45.
Monday, 9-19-22

> God's will - nothing more, nothing less,
nothing else.   — on a plaque hanging
                          in G. Campbell Morgan's
(From Glad Tidings   study
program, Dr. J. Allen Blair
on BBN radio — 107.1 FM/WYFA
6:30 A.M. (DST); Topic - A plan for receiving God's
                                   guidance)
> Pss. 70 & 40, plus commentary
from The Light of the Psalms: Deepening your
faith with every Psalm, Michael F. Ross
Psalm 40 hymn — I Waited for the Lord my God;
413 in The Hymnbook (1912 Psalter)
Ps. 69 — Hymn 393 — Thy Loving-kindness, Lord,
is Good and Free

I delight to do Your will, O my God,
And Your law is within my heart.

PSALM 40:8 NKJV

Take Time

Intimacy may not be rushed.... We can't dash into God's presence
and choke down spiritual inwardness before we hurry
to our one o'clock appointment. Inwardness is time-consuming,
open only to minds willing to sample spirituality in small bites,
savoring each one.

CALVIN MILLER

It may seem strange to think that God wants to spend time with us,
but...think about it. If God went to all the trouble to come to earth,
to live the life that He did, to die for us, then there's got to be a hunger
and a passion behind that. We think of prayer as an "ought to,"
but in reality it is a response to God's passionate love for us.
We need to refocus on the fact that God is waiting for us to show up
and be with Him and that our presence truly touches Him.

DR. HENRY CLOUD

Come and sit and ask Him whatever is on your heart.
No question is too small, no riddle too simple.
He has all the time in the world.
Come and seek the will of God.

MAX LUCADO

Thursday, 9-22-22

> Help me, Lord my God; save me according to
your faithful love. - Psalm 109:26 HCSB
(From A Daily Journey through Psalms for Women, 2012;
Day 265: If You Become Discouraged) / ISBN
978-1-60587-451-7 (Brentwood, Tennessee:
Freeman - Smith, a division of Worthy
Media, Inc.)

> Proverbs 22:24-25 (NLT) - Keep away from angry,
short -tempered people, or you will learn to be
like them and endanger your soul.

> Voices of the Saints, Bert Ghezzi -232,
Malachy (1098-1148), pp. 464-5; reported
by Bernard as instrumental in providing inner
healing for woman known for having a
temper problem. St. B. thought it of
greater consequence than Malachy's having
raised a dead woman to physical life.

> Choose a good reputation over great riches, for
being held in high esteem is better than having
silver or gold.   - Proverbs 22:1 (NLT)

I've loved you the way my Father has loved me.
Make yourselves at home in my love.

JOHN 15:9 MSG

He Comes in Stillness

He doesn't come in the roaring thunder, as we expect.
He doesn't write in blazing lightning as it flashes across the clouds,
even though we watch for Him there. His voice won't be in
the rushing wind or in the pounding rhythm of the waves breaking
against the seashore. He simply comes to us in a still small voice.

WENDY MOORE

We may ask, "Why does God bring thunderclouds and disasters
when we want green pastures and still waters?" Bit by bit,
we find behind the clouds, the Father's feet; behind the lightning,
an abiding day that has no night; behind the thunder, a still small voice
that comforts with a comfort that is unspeakable.

OSWALD CHAMBERS

"Go out, and stand on the mountain before the LORD."
And behold, the LORD passed by, and a great and strong wind
tore into the mountains..., but the LORD was not in the wind;
and after the wind an earthquake, but the LORD was not
in the earthquake; and after the earthquake a fire, but the LORD
was not in the fire; and after the fire a still small voice.

1 KINGS 19:11–12 NKJV

Sat., 9-24-22
> <u>Daily Light</u> (Bagster/Lotz) - Heb. 10:19-22
(Sept. 24; Oct. 18; Dec. 18 - Morning); Heb. 13:6
(Oct. 8; Dec. 18 - Morning)
Sun., 9-25-22
> <u>Turning Points</u>, David Jeremiah - "Imperfections
Made Perfect," 2 Cor. 12:9; Rom. 8:28;
(September 25, p. 280); (Brentwood, Tennessee:
Integrity Publishers, 2005) / ISBN 1-59145-067-5
(hardcover)

Mon. & Tues., 9-26/27/2022
> <u>Start Late, Finish Rich</u>, David Bach
> <u>Voices of the Saints</u>, ~~Bob~~ Bert Ghezzi: September 27 -
• Vincent de Paul (1581-1660), patron of charitable
societies; collaborator, c̄ St. Louise de Marillac,
in founding the Sisters of Charity
• March 15 - Louise de Marillac (1591-1660), patron
of social workers; Sisters of Charity founded in 1633.
Corresponded with friend about relaxing perfectionistic
bent.

The lightning and thunder, they go and they come,
But the stars and the stillness are always at home.

GEORGE MACDONALD

God Is Great

The simple fact of being...in the presence of the Lord
and of showing Him all that I think, feel, sense, and experience,
without trying to hide anything, must please Him. Somehow,
somewhere, I know that He loves me, even though I do not feel
that love as I can feel a human embrace, even though I do not hear
a voice as I hear human words of consolation.... God is greater
than my senses, greater than my thoughts, greater than my heart.
I do believe that He touches me in places
that are unknown even to myself.

HENRI J. M. NOUWEN

Have you ever thought what a wonderful privilege it is that
every one each day and each hour of the day has the liberty of asking
God to meet him in the inner chamber and to hear what He has to say?

ANDREW MURRAY

The LORD your God is with you....
He will take great delight in you,
he will quiet you with his love,
he will rejoice over you with singing.

ZEPHANIAH 3:17 NIV

Wed., 9-28-2022
> Daily Light (Bagster/Lotz) – Num. 6:27 ... Prov. 18:10
> Days of Praise (Sept. 28, 2006) – "the Christian's
Parentage," Eph. 2:1; Rom. 3:10-11; I Cor. 2:14;
Eph. 2:2; Gal. 4:3; II Cor. 4:4; Eph. 2:3; 5:5-6;
John 3:36; Rom. 2:5-9; Eph. 2:10,4; John 5:21-24;
Rom. 6:4-6, 9-11; Eph. 2:6, 8-9; Rom. 8:29-39;
Eph. 2:7. (-Henry M. Morris III, D.Min.)
> BBN Radio, 7:10 A.M. - ~~instrumental~~ orchestral version of
And Can It Be, featuring wind instrument
(oboe, clarinet?) / announcer, S. Brown
Thursday, 9-29-22   on BBN radio:
   C.S. Lewis, writing to a child —   Ch. 17, C.S.
                                          Lewis: Apostle
   Only three things need be done: to the Skeptics
                                          (Moody Radio)
1) Things we ought to do;   ... be kind ...
2)   "   we've got to do;   ... buy groceries ...
3)   "   we like to do.   ... what do you like doing?   be
                                                              praying
Also responded to another (American) child   I'll for you; do
                                              please pray
about how to become a writer. First, turn off the   for me,
                                                     too.
radio. Don't make writing your only interest,
or you'll have nothing to write about. Read much, but
                                         not many magazines
 God is the sunshine that warms us, the rain that melts the frost   & more--
    and waters the young plants. The presence of God   a lengthy
    is a climate of strong and bracing love, always there.   reply,

                        JOAN ARNOLD

He's Near

The God who made the world and everything in it, this Master of sky
and land, doesn't live in custom-made shrines or need the human race
to run errands for him, as if he couldn't take care of himself. He makes
the creatures; the creatures don't make him. Starting from scratch,
he made the entire human race and made the earth hospitable,
with plenty of time and space for living so we could seek after God,
and not just grope around in the dark but actually find him.
He doesn't play hide-and-seek with us. He's not remote; he's near.

ACTS 17:24–27 MSG

God is not an elusive dream or a phantom to chase,
but a divine person to know. He does not avoid us, but seeks us.
When we seek Him, the contact is instantaneous.

NEVA COYLE

God proves to be good to the man who passionately waits,
to the woman who diligently seeks.
It's a good thing to quietly hope,
quietly hope for help from God.

LAMENTATIONS 3:25–26 MSG

Oct. 3, 2022
Focus on the Family - Dr. Bill Lyle with
clarifying info. re: health care and
abortion. Example given to debunk
fake news about ectopic pregnancies.
Oct. 5, 2022 (Wed.)
Point of View - intv. with Col. Alan West
   ACRU - American Constitution Restoration

Oct. 11, 2022 (Tues.)
On Glen Beck - John Sullivan, Nothing But News
(re: Ukraine)

Oct. 15, 2022
→ The Sontino Books - 14-book/volume commentary on
the Jewish scriptures, recommended by Charlie Dyer
during Q+A section of The Land and the Book
(91.7 FM - WLPE)

Mon., 10-17-22
› Daily Light (Bagster Lhotz) - Morning: 1 Peter 1:8
et al.
› Turning Points (David Jeremiah) - Oct. 17: "Get Back
to Work;" John 21:15b

To seek God means first of all
to let yourself be found by Him.

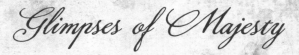

Glimpses of Majesty

Worship the LORD in the splendor of his holiness;
tremble before him, all the earth.
Say among the nations, "The LORD reigns."
The world is firmly established, it cannot be moved;
he will judge the peoples with equity.
Let the heavens rejoice, let the earth be glad;
let the sea resound, and all that is in it;
let the fields be jubilant, and everything in them.
Then all the trees of the forest will sing for joy

PSALM 96:9–12 NIV

Forbid that I should walk through
Thy beautiful world with unseeing eyes:
Forbid that the lure of the market-place
should ever entirely steal my heart away from
the love of the open acres and the green trees:
Forbid that under the low roof of workshop
or office or study I should ever forget
Thy great overarching sky.

JOHN BAILLIE

The God who holds the whole world in His hands
wraps Himself in the splendor of the sun's light
and walks among the clouds.

Oct. 17, 2022 (Monday)

> BBN Radio's Musical Backgrounds - from _Hymn Histories_ by Alfred B. Smith, a Charles Gabriel hymn, "the Glory Song" (O That Will Be Glory); inspired by Ed Card, whose spiritual transformation led him from being sullen and dull to reflecting God's glory to such an extent that he became known as "the glory man."

> Proverbs 15:15, 19

Oct. 18, 2022 (Tuesday)

From 1 Thess. 4, comfort for mourners:
God will bring with Jesus those who have fallen asleep. (v.14)
They will rise first ~~with~~ at his descent, ~~at the~~ with his command, ~~and with~~ an archangel's voice, and God's ~~trumpet~~ sound. (v.16)
We will rise with them ^in the clouds^, meet him ^in the air^, and always be with him. (v.17)

Oct. 27, 2022

Money Wise on WLPE-91.7 FM
Intv. with author (and financial columnist for _The Christian Post_ Jerry Bower (Bauer?)). Wrote the book _The Makers and the Takers_. Recommends return to work for early retirees and recognizing that the fourth commandment calls not only for a day of rest but also six days of work.

_S_avor little glimpses of God's goodness and His majesty, thankful for the gift of them.

Desert Bloom

The desert and the parched land will be glad;
the wilderness will rejoice and blossom.
Like the crocus, it will burst into bloom;
it will rejoice greatly and shout for joy....
They will see the glory of the LORD,
the splendor of our God....
Then will the eyes of the blind be opened
and the ears of the deaf unstopped.
Then will the lame leap like a deer,
and the mute tongue shout for joy.
Water will gush forth in the wilderness
and streams in the desert.

ISAIAH 35:1–2, 5–6 NIV

Every journey has a wilderness passage. Sometimes quite a few.
But as the path leads on, we discover that without the desert,
we do not fully experience the oasis.

BARBARA FARMER

See, I am doing a new thing!
Now it springs up; do you not perceive it?
I am making a way in the desert
and streams in the wasteland.

ISAIAH 43:19 NIV

Thursday, Nov. 3, 2022
> Hymn : O Master, Let Me Walk with Thee (Gladden / Smith)
> Daily Light (Bagster ; Lotz) – November 3 / Morning :
    Hosea 14:9 ... John 10:27; incl. Matt. 6:22
> Acts 20:7-12 ; 3:1-10
> Whispers of Friendship (Barbour Publshrs.) –
    Day 307 – Divine Vitality : Lydia Maria
    Childs quote re : working miracles thru love
> Faith's Checkbook (Spurgeon), Nov. 3 – In God's Divine
    Time ; Habakkuk 2:3
> Look Unto Me : The Devotions of Charles Spurgeon
    (Ed., Reimann) – Nov. 3; Acts 9:11 – God loves
    to hear us ; includes Joseph Parker quote, expanded
    by Reimann. Parker was contemporary of Spurgeon.
    Our prayers are "fragrant."
    Friday, 11-04-22
> One Day At a Time (MacDonald), p. 322 (Nov. 4)
(NKJV) 1 John 3:10 ; also, 4:2 ; 5:1 ; 5:2 ; 2:10 ;
    3:10, 14 ; 4:7, 12 ; 3:24 ; 3:6, 9 ; 5:18 ; 2:29 ;
    3:7 ; 2:15.
                                    many
                                    false prophets
                                    love made
                                    complete
(NIV) Cf. 1 John 2:2, 8, 17, 18-27 ; 3:8b, 14b, 24b ; 4:1c, 12,
    14, 20b-21 ; 5:2 (5:1-5), 6 (baptism & crucifixion), 20.
          "I write these things..." – vv. 2:1a, 26 ; 5:13
        Within each of us, just waiting to blossom,
        is the wonderful promise of all we can be.

Fully Satisfied

O God, you are my God;
I earnestly search for you.
My soul thirsts for you;
my whole body longs for you
in this parched and weary land
where there is no water.
I have seen you in your sanctuary
and gazed upon your power and glory.
Your unfailing love is better than life itself....
I will praise you as long as I live.

PSALM 63:1–4 NLT

The Lord's chief desire is to reveal Himself to you and, in order for
Him to do that, He gives you abundant grace. The Lord gives you the
experience of enjoying His presence. He touches you, and His touch is
so delightful that, more than ever, you are drawn inwardly to Him.

MADAME JEANNE GUYON

Blessed are those who hunger and thirst for righteousness,
for they will be filled.

MATTHEW 5:6 NIV

Genuine heart-hunger, accompanied by sincere seeking
after eternal values, does not go unrewarded.

JUSTINE KNIGHT

Friday, 11-04-22
> Gal. 4:1-5 -- ~~good~~ Christmas passage
> Anthem - All That Is You, Is All that We Need;
  based on Philippians 4:8
> Hymn - O God, Thou Art the Father (No. 93 in
The ~~Hymnal~~; Columba (521-597); Trans. by
Duncan ~~McGregor~~ Macgregor (1854-1923);
DURROW: 7.6.7.6. D. / Traditional Irish melody]
Sat., 11-05-22
I've been set free in Christ Jesus from the
law of sin and death, thru the Spirit of
life. (Rom. 8:2 Jn)
Sunday, 11-06-2022
> Song: Jesus, be the Lord of me
         Jesus, be the Lord of all the kingdoms of
         my heart
> ~~Whispers of Friendship~~ (Barbour Pub.) - "The Best
Things," Robert Louis Stevenson, #310, ^{Day} p.
Reminds me of Elisabeth*Elliot's advice on
depression; she says, "Do the next thing." (source?)
R.L.S. says the best things are nearest, including
"the path of God just before you."

Only God can fully satisfy the hungry heart.

HUGH BLACK

Experience Christ

I pray that from his glorious, unlimited resources he will empower you
with inner strength through his Spirit. Then Christ will make his home
in your hearts as you trust in him. Your roots will grow down into
God's love and keep you strong. And may you have the power
to understand, as all God's people should, how wide, how long,
how high, and how deep his love is. May you experience
the love of Christ, though it is too great to understand fully.
Then you will be made complete with all the fullness of life
and power that comes from God.

EPHESIANS 3:16–19 NLT

Let us continue to love each other since love comes from God.
Everyone who loves is born of God
and experiences a relationship with God.

1 JOHN 4:7 MSG

Once the seeking heart finds God in personal experience
there will be no problem about loving Him. To know Him
is to love Him and to know Him better is to love Him more.

A. W. TOZER

Monday, 11-07-2022
> Hymns - Jesus Calls Us; O Thou, In Whose Presence;
O Bread of Life, for All Men Broken (450 in
The Hymnal) - words by Timothy T'ingfang Lew, 1936;
Trans. by Frank W. Price, 1952; alt. /Tune: SHENG EN/
Music by Su ~~Yin-Lan~~ Yin-lan, 1934; Arr. by
Bliss Wiant, 1936; alt., 1953. Music from Hymns of
Universal Praise.
Tues., 11-08-22
> Family Talk with Dr. James Dobson
   Conversation c̄ Harvard-trained sociolgist-
researcher & author Shante Felhan. Part 1 of 2-part
broadcast. Most recent book, co-authored c̄ husband, Jeff:
Thriving in Love and Money. Wrote two books herself also-
For Men Only and For Women Only.
>   John Barnett - "A Grace-Energized Woman
   Is Discreet;" sermon heard on BBN's Building
Blocks for the Family -- good for all, not only
~~women~~.   Titus 2:12; Phil. 4:8; 2 Tim. 1:7
(Like the way he preaches.)

This is how we know what love is:
Jesus Christ laid down his life for us.

1 JOHN 3:16 NIV

He Restores My Soul

The LORD is my shepherd, I shall not be in want.
He makes me lie down in green pastures,
he leads me beside quiet waters,
he restores my soul.
He guides me in paths of righteousness
for his name's sake.
Even though I walk
through the valley of the shadow of death,
I will fear no evil,
for you are with me;
your rod and your staff,
they comfort me.
You prepare a table before me
in the presence of my enemies.
You anoint my head with oil;
my cup overflows.
Surely goodness and love will follow me
all the days of my life,
and I will dwell in the house of the LORD
forever.

PSALM 23:1–6 NIV

The purpose of grace is primarily to restore our relationship
with God.... This is what all the work of grace aims at—an ever deeper
knowledge of God, and an ever closer fellowship with Him.

J. I. PACKER

My people will dwell in a peaceful habitation,
In secure dwellings, and in quiet resting places.

ISAIAH 32:18 NKJV

Sunday, 11-13-2022

> <u>Christian Brotherhood Newsletter</u> (mentioned as
alternative to medical insurance[*] by Franklin E.
Payne, Jr., M.D. in his book <u>Biblical Healing for
Modern Medicine</u>) (Augusta, GA : Covenant Books,
1993) ; pp. 175; 72 [68;71]. Christian Brotherhood Newsletter,
P.O. Box 832, Barberton, Ohio 44203; phone (216)
848-1511. [*]Takes into account the impact of
morality on personal health. Not an insurance
program, but gateway to expense-sharing among
believers.

> Hymn: Softly Now the Light of Day
    Four verses, no. 60 in <u>The Hymnal</u>
    George W. Doane, 1824 / (1799-1859)[*]
    SEYMOUR : 7.7.7.7
    Arr. from Carl M. von Weber, 1826 / (1786-1826)[*]
[*](Also in Worship and Service Hymnal, no. 143);
    Alternate tune : MERCY; I prefer SEYMOUR.

*𝒴ou have made us for Thyself, O Lord; and our hearts
are restless until they find rest in Thee.*

AUGUSTINE (Gerhard Tersteegen,
originally?)

Moments to Reflect

Much of what is sacred is hidden in the ordinary,
everyday moments of our lives. To see something of the sacred
in those moments takes slowing down
so we can live our lives more reflectively.

KEN GIRE

Reflection...enables our minds to be stretched
in three different directions—the direction that leads
to a proper relationship with God, the relationship that leads
to a healthy relationship with others, and the relationship
that leads to a deeper understanding of oneself.

MARK CONNOLLY

What we lack is not so much leisure to do as time to reflect
and time to feel. What we seldom "take" is time to experience
the things that have happened, the things that are happening,
the things that are still ahead of us.

MARGARET MEAD & RHODA METRAUX

What we feel, think, and do this moment influences
both our present and the future in ways we may never know.
Begin. Start right where you are.

ALEXANDRA STODDARD

Sunday, 11-13-22

> Hymn: With Thankful Hearts, O Lord, We Come
(no. 516 in _Worship and Service Hymnal_); 4 vss.
J.S. Mohler, 19th Century (words)
TUNE: MOHLER (L.M. 8,8,8,8)
J. Henry Showalter, 1864-1947

Monday, 11-14-22

> BBN's Words of Praise (Dr. Donald R. Hubbard) 5:30 A.M.
Acts 4:23 ff
Divine
∧Impact equation = People, Prayer, Power (H.S.),
                          Possessions, Participation
Justified people* are the people who make a lasting
impact. (by grace, thru faith in the Lord Jesus Christ)
Unified together in love ("they"...)
Followed by:
- I Must Tell Jesus; Praise Ye the Lord   (Ed Phillips
                                          hosting /announcer)
- Warren Wiersbe: "To be heavenly-minded simply means
to look at earth from heaven's point of view." (More
quoted from recent msg. -- incl. something about
making an impact, I think.)

God Wants You

Listening to God is a firsthand experience.... God invites *you*
to vacation in His splendor. He invites *you* to feel the touch of His hand.
He invites *you* to feast at His table. He wants to spend time with *you*.

MAX LUCADO

The Most High calls to us and waits for us to respond.
He desires to quench our deepest thirst, to satisfy our deepest hunger,
and to fill us with His power and presence as we dwell
in the secret place of the Most High.

CYNTHIA HEALD

He is a God who can be found. A God who can be known.
A God who wants to be close to us. That's why He is called Immanuel,
which means "God with us." But He draws close to us
as we draw close to Him.

STORMIE OMARTIAN

Come near to God and he will come near to you.

JAMES 4:8 NIV

17-

Thurs./Fri. - Nov. 18, 2022

> His truth be thine affiance when faint and
   desolate.

> Eph. 6:12 ff; 1 Jn. 2:16 (lust of flesh & eyes, pride of life)
   Three enemies: the world, the flesh, the Devil

> Dr. R.C. McQuilken's two daily questions:
   1) Am I totally committed to do only God's will? (Obey)
   2) Am I in a position to believe? (Trust)

> Romans 8:31b, and its corollary; example of Job

Sat., 11-19-22

First Person Interview (.com) on 91.7FM-WLPE @ 2:25p

Love Packages.org   Steve Schmidt

   Butler, Ill. & Decatur, Ala. warehouses (plus collection
   Ship Christian lit. overseas   points across the
                                            country)

Sunday, 11-20-22   (evening)

> Thru the Bible: Sunday Sermon, J. Vernon McGee
   Church of the Open Door, Los Angeles, Calif.
   Romans 2:11,12 - What About the Heathen?
   Evangelism starts where you are. Don't have to
   go overseas. Hymn: Wonderful Saviour (J.M.
   Harris; Praise and Worship Hymnal, no. 20; Kansas
   City, MO: Lillenas Publishing Company; Date Unknown)

*G*od is always speaking to us. Listen to Him.
He wants from us deep love, compassion, and forgiveness.

MOTHER TERESA

Through His Creation

In such a beautiful wilderness of wildflowers we are amused with the
very variety and novelty of the scene so much that we in our pleasure
lose all sense of weariness or fatigue in the length of our wanderings
and get to the end before we are aware of our journey.

JOHN CLARE

God's love is like a river springing up in the Divine Substance
and flowing endlessly through His creation,
filling all things with life and goodness and strength.

THOMAS MERTON

I am convinced that God has built into all of us an appreciation
of beauty and has even allowed us to participate in the creation
of beautiful things and places. It may be one way God brings healing
to our brokenness, and a way that we can contribute toward
bringing wholeness to our fallen world.

MARY JANE WORDEN

Our Creator would never have made such lovely days,
and have given us the deep hearts to enjoy them,
above and beyond all thought,
unless we were meant to be immortal.

NATHANIEL HAWTHORNE

Friday, Nov. 25, 2022
> 1 Chronicles 21:15; 22:19a
Sat., Nov. 26, 2022
> 1 Chr. 22:9-10 (Ck. ESV footnotes)
Sun., 11-27-22
> Mike Mason's _The Gospel According to Job_ --
   Luck (Job 1:21b); pp. 39-40
   Trouble from God (Job 2:10); pp. 47-48 (incl. quote from King George VI's 1940 radio talk)
   Nakedness (Job 1:21a); pp. 37-8 (God not only loves his people -- he likes them. Do we like him?)
> (Review prompted by verses from Job brought to mind
   while reading Dr. David Jeremiah's devotional
   titled "Now Thank We All Our God" in his _Turning_
   Points devotional book; Nov. ~~24~~ 25; p. 344.)   Martin-Reinkart-Eilenberg, Saxony
> _The Gift of Obedience: A Practical Study on God's_
   Law by Steve Brown (~~pamphlet~~ booklet) -- concludes
   with Mother Teresa quote: "O God, teach me to
   love you even if there is no heaven ... and teach
   me to fear you even if there is no hell."
> _The Parables of Peanuts_, Robert L. Short - pages 296-310
   in last chapter: Slip-ups, Doghouses, and Free ₿ Psychia-
   tric Help. (New York, NY: Harper Collins Publishers, Inc., 2002)
   Ends with quotation from Charles Schultz commencement
   address re: Peter's restoration. John 21:15-17

𝓗onor and majesty surround him;
strength and beauty fill his sanctuary.

PSALM 96:6 NLT

An Invitation

Are you tired? Worn out? Burned out on religion? Come to me.
Get away with me and you'll recover your life. I'll show you
how to take a real rest. Walk with me and work with me—
watch how I do it. Learn the unforced rhythms of grace.
I won't lay anything heavy or ill-fitting on you. Keep company with me
and you'll learn to live freely and lightly.

MATTHEW 11:28–30 MSG

[God] is looking for people who will come in simple dependence
upon His grace, and rest in simple faith upon His greatness.
At this very moment, He's looking at you.

JACK HAYFORD

Come, all you who are thirsty,
come to the waters;
and you who have no money,
come, buy and eat!
Come, buy wine and milk
without money and without cost.
Why spend money on what is not bread,
and your labor on what does not satisfy?
Listen, listen to me, and eat what is good,
and your soul will delight in the richest of fare.
Give ear and come to me;
hear me, that your soul may live.

ISAIAH 55:1–3 NIV

Tues., 11-29-22
> 1 Chronicles 27:32^a - Jonathan, David's uncle -
a man of understanding and a scribe -
a counselor. (32b - he "attended the king's
sons"); v. 33a - Ahithophel, king's counselor;
v. 33b - Hushai (the Archite), king's friend.
See also v. 34 - counselor successors;
army commander (Joab).
> 2 Peter 1:17 - the Father well-pleased in the
Son (@ Jesus' transfiguration)
> The Church's One Foundation - Samuel Johnstone
wrote, based on The Apostle's Creed (east-end
Brit & pastor who worked with his pastor
father; music by Charles Wesley's grandson
Samuel, once known as Britain's greatest
church organist). From Musical Memos by
Lindsey Terry (Daniels Publishing); aired 7 P.M.
Tues., 11-29-22 on BBN's Musical Backgrounds.

Come with me by yourselves to a quiet place and get some rest.

MARK 6:31 NIV

God Is for Us

Don't be afraid, I've redeemed you.
I've called your name. You're mine.
When you're in over your head, I'll be there with you.
When you're in rough waters, you will not go down.
When you're between a rock and a hard place,
it won't be a dead end—
Because I am God, your personal God,
The Holy One of Israel, your Savior.
I paid a huge price for you...!
That's how much you mean to me!
That's how much I love you!

ISAIAH 43:1–4 MSG

Our days are filled with tiny golden minutes with eternity in them.
Our lives are immortal. One thousand years from this day you will be
more alive than you are at this moment. There is a future life with God
for those who put their trust in Him.

BILLY GRAHAM

Let him who walks in the dark,
who has no light,
trust in the name of the LORD
and rely on his God.

ISAIAH 50:10 NIV

2 Peter 1:16-21

Tue., 12/06/22
> 2 Chronicles 5:11 6:36a
Friday, 12/09/22
> God loves me.
  God knows better than me.
  God is in control.
  God is good.
Wed., 12-21-2022
GNN Radio 91.7 FM
> R.C. Murrow – (Prophecy Tracker. org)
Heard discussing monetary policy with Rick DeYoung
on Prophecy Today (re: Pres. Biden instructing
Federal Reserve to move from paper money to
digital currency).
> Point of View (.net)
   GAP Program – 9 mos., for young people transitioning
   to adulthood. Denton Bible Church – Dallas, TX
   "Combination Green Beret, Boy Scouts, Seminary"
   Tommy Elson; Drew and Christy
   Denton.Bible.org
   Mentors and regular evaluation (about once a month)

*I*f God is for us, who can be against us?

ROMANS 8:31 NKJV

Wait for the Promises

We must wait for God, long, meekly, in the wind and wet,
in the thunder and lightning, in the cold and the dark.
Wait, and He will come.

FREDERICK W. FABER

Peace does not dwell in outward things but in the heart prepared
to wait trustfully and quietly on Him who has all things safely
in His hands.... Jesus had perfect trust in His Father, whose will
He had come to accomplish. Nothing touched Him without
His Father's permission. Nothing touches me without
my Father's permission. Can I not then wait patiently?
He will show the way.

ELISABETH ELLIOT

A wise gardener plants his seeds, then has the good sense
not to dig them up every few days to see if a crop is on the way.
Likewise, we must be patient as God brings the answers...
in His own good time.

QUIN SHERRER

The Scriptures give us hope and encouragement as we wait patiently
for God's promises to be fulfilled.

ROMANS 15:4 NLT

The way may at times seem dark, but light will arise,
if you trust in the Lord, and wait patiently for Him.

ELIZABETH T. KING

Thursday, Dec. 22, 2022
> Luke 11:27, 28, 35
> National School Chaplain Association.org
  (1st hr. – 2nd half hr. intv. on Point of View
   with Kerby Anderson; Point of View.net)
Monday, 12-26-22
> Point of View c̄ Kerby Anderson (2nd hr.)
  Author intv. – Jeff Myers, Ph.D., author of
  Truth Changes Everything; also works with
  Summit Ministries.
  "If you want to . . .
   " "   " " change a decade, plant a tree.
   " "   " "   "   , teach a child the
      unreasonable virtues : faith, hope, and love.
  Quote from . . . (?)
  Truth = reality ; it's alive, it's eten eternal.
  (Same intv. also aired Nov. 23, 2022.)
> The Valley of Vision
   - The Infinite and the Finite, pp. 190-191 (4: NEEDS AND DEVOTIONS)
   - Calvary's Anthem, pp. 314-5 (7: GIFTS OF GRACE)

God makes a promise—faith believes it,
hope anticipates it, patience quietly awaits it.

You Satisfy My Soul

In comparison with this big world, the human heart is only
a small thing. Though the world is so large, it is utterly unable
to satisfy this tiny heart. Our ever growing soul and its capacities
can be satisfied only in the infinite God. As water is restless until
it reaches its level, so the soul has no peace until it rests in God.

SADHU SUNDAR SINGH

Whom have I in heaven but you?
And earth has nothing I desire besides you.
My flesh and my heart may fail,
but God is the strength of my heart
and my portion forever.

PSALM 73:25–26 NIV

God bless you and utterly satisfy your heart...with Himself.

AMY CARMICHAEL

They shall neither hunger nor thirst,
Neither heat nor sun shall strike them;
For He who has mercy on them will lead them,
Even by the springs of water He will guide them.

ISAIAH 49:10 NKJV

We are made for God, and nothing less will really satisfy us.

BRENNAN MANNING

Monday, 12-26-22

> Voices of the Saints, Bert Ghezzi
  - John Neumann : called as a missionary to N. Amer.;
    arrived in New York (Buffalo - Rochester), 1836.
  - Marguerite D'Youville : ~~suffered~~ had many troubles;
    became minister to the poor in Montreal after
    husband's death; formalized her group as Sisters
    of Charity (a.k.a. Grey Sisters)/wore gray habits;
    esp. served Inuits of N. America.
  - Frances Xavier Cabrini (1850 - 1917), pp. 228-29
    See letter she wrote to a sister prone to melancholy,
    1885. Excellent counsel! 1880 - mssys. of
    the Sacred Heart established - education, nursing,
    care of orphans; eight countries, including
    America (N.Y., New Orleans, Chicago), Nicaragua
    (Managua), Argentina (Buenos Aires). She herself
    was from Italy and had planned to become a mssy.
    to China from childhood, but was never led there.
    Became U.S. citizen & first canonized American
    saint.

*J*esus said, "I am the Bread of Life. The person who aligns with me
hungers no more and thirsts no more, ever."

JOHN 6:35 MSG

A Quiet Spirit

Don't ever let yourself get so busy that you miss those little
but important extras in life—the beauty of a day...the smile of a friend...
the serenity of a quiet moment alone. For it is often life's
smallest pleasures and gentlest joys that make the biggest
and most lasting difference.

A quiet place is a good place to find out God's angle on any problem.

JANETTE OKE

Don't be concerned about the outward beauty of fancy hairstyles,
expensive jewelry, or beautiful clothes. You should clothe yourselves
instead with the beauty that comes from within, the unfading beauty
of a gentle and quiet spirit, which is so precious to God.

1 PETER 3:3–4 NLT

Year by year the complexities of this spinning world grow
more bewildering, and so each year we need all the more
to seek peace and comfort in the joyful simplicities.

He who dwells in the secret place of the Most High
Shall abide under the shadow of the Almighty.
I will say of the LORD, "He is my refuge and my fortress;
My God, in Him I will trust."

PSALM 91:1–2 NKJV

Tues., 12/27/2022

> Glad Tidings with Dr. J. Allen Blair (6:30 A.M., 107.1
FM / BBN Radio; avail. on ~~demand~~ demand)
On judicious use of speech – very good
Incl. quote of something St. Augustine is
said to have displayed at his dinner table
re: no slander of persons absent

Wed., 12/28/2022

> Voices of the Saints, Bert Ghezzi

> No. 272 – Nicholas of Flue (Switzerland) / 1417 – 1487,
pp. 544-5 (March 22); "Saints and Politics;" "Married
Saints."
Source: Marie McSwigan's Athlete of Christ
(Westminster, Maryland: The Newman Press, 1959.),
p. 776 in Ghezzi.

> No. 37 – Bede (673-735) – England. Wrote 25
commentaries and History of the English Church and
People. Known as Venerable Bede; May 25; pp. 74-5.
Explained & used fourfold method of Scripture
interpretation: history, tropology, allegory,
anagogy.

Depths of the Spirit

"No eye has seen, no ear has heard, no mind has conceived
what God has prepared for those who love him"—
but God has revealed it to us by his Spirit. The Spirit searches all things,
even the deep things of God. For who among men knows the thoughts
of a man except the man's spirit within him? In the same way no one
knows the thoughts of God except the Spirit of God. We have not
received the spirit of the world but the Spirit who is from God,
that we may understand what God has freely given us.

1 CORINTHIANS 2:9–12 NIV

Praise is a place for God to be. A home place. A workshop
for His Holy Spirit in our lives. It is an atmosphere of total openness
where He can be free to do good things in and through our days.

GLORIA GAITHER

The grace of the Lord Jesus Christ, and the love of God,
and the communion of the Holy Spirit be with you all. Amen.

2 CORINTHIANS 13:14 NKJV

Mon., Jan. 16, 2023
David Jeremiah (radio spot on GNN Radio, 3:30 P.M.)
Samuel Wilberforce ~~orce~~, 19th Cent. Anglican bishop, on the
1) admit   four features of the Christian Life :
2) submit
3) commit
4) transmit

Point of View, 2nd hr. (.net)
Intv. with musician & author, Ron Block (.com)
Abiding Dependence : Living Moment   Blue Grass - does
                      By Moment in   banjo & guitar
Moody Publishers   the Love of God   workshops
(Forty days of devotions) / forty chapters

Wed., 1-18-23
> Morning hymns :
 - Lord, Speak to Me / CANONBURY - Frances R. Havergal
    and Robert Schumann (19th Cent.); 338 in Worship
    and Service Hymnal

*God knows the rhythm of my spirit
and knows my heart thoughts.
He is as close as breathing.*

Sanctuary of the Soul

Deep within us all there is an amazing inner sanctuary of the soul,
a holy place, a Divine Center, a speaking Voice, to which
we may continuously return. Eternity is at our hearts,
pressing upon our time-torn lives, warming us with intimations
of an astounding destiny, calling us home unto Itself.

THOMAS R. KELLY

The soul is like a wild animal—tough, resilient, resourceful,
savvy, self-sufficient. It knows how to survive in hard places.
But it is also shy. Just like a wild animal, it seeks safety
in the dense underbrush. If we want to see a wild animal,
we know that the last thing we should do is go crashing through the
woods yelling for it to come out. But if we will walk quietly
into the woods, sit patiently by the base of the tree, and fade into
our surroundings, the wild animal we seek might put in an appearance.

PARKER PALMER

As for God, his way is perfect;
the word of the LORD is flawless.
He is a shield for all who take refuge in him.

PSALM 18:30 NIV

Wed., 1-18-23
> Morning hymns :
- The Name of Jesus (W.C. Martin /Edmund S. Lorenz);
  286 in Crowning Glory Hymnal (Grand Rapids, Michigan:
  Singspiration, Inc., by Zondervan Publishing House;
  1964)
- Every Bridge Is Burned Behind Me (Johnson Oatman, Jr. /
  Geo. C. Hugg); 116 in Praise and Worship Hymnal
  (Kansas City, Missouri: Lillenas Publishing Company;
  Date unknown); from Athens Church of the Nazarene,
  Nazarene Publishing House* per dedication sticker
  * Kansas City, Missouri

Thursday, Jan. 19, 2023
> Hymn : Saviour, Thy Dying Love / TUNE : SOMETHING FOR THEE
  (Sylvanus D. Phelps / Robert Lowry; Descant, William Lester)
  334 in Worship and Service Hymnal; four verses (Carol
  Stream, Illinois: Hope Publishing Company, 1957)

*W*ithin each of us there is an inner place where the
living God Himself longs to dwell, our sacred center of belief.

Whispered Prayer

We do not need to search for heaven, over here or over there,
in order to find our eternal Father. In fact, we do not even need to
speak out loud, for though we speak in the smallest whisper
or the most fleeting thought, He is close enough to hear us.

TERESA OF AVILA

We can go through all the activities of our days in joyful awareness
of God's presence with whispered prayers of praise and adoration
flowing continuously from our hearts.

RICHARD J. FOSTER

I need not shout my faith. Thrice eloquent
Are quiet trees and the green listening sod;
Hushed are the stars, whose power is never spent;
The hills are mute: yet how they speak of God!

CHARLES HANSON TOWNE

God doesn't need us to shout.
We can whisper and He still hears our prayers.

GARY SMALLEY AND JOHN TRENT

There is a time for everything, and a season
for every activity under heaven...
a time to be silent and a time to speak.

ECCLESIASTES 3:1, 7 NIV

Fri., 1-20-23

> Prophecy Today - Jimmy De Young Jr. - speaking to Mike ?
  Info. about Roman Catholicism's future plans

> Proclaiming the Gospel. com - Mike ?   (taken from
                                                          their official
- R.C. is amillenial - denies literal   website)
    thousand years   RomanCatholicism.org

- Also denies rapture due to teaching about purgatory
  → offers mthly. newsletter   - One world religion
                                      push (works-related)
                                    - R.C. world leader
                                      expectation (= the
                                      anti-Christ)

> Reading on WLPE/91.7FM @ 5:10 P.M., from
  Rock Int'l.'s book, The King of Glory. Story
  of Senegalese believer, Malik, who's worked
  among the Wolof* for Christ. Book avail. thru
  GNN Radio.

Sat., 1-21-23
> Prov. 16:32; 21:3; Isa. 26; Hosea 6

Every whispered prayer sent heavenward
is our response to God's embrace.

JANET L. WEAVER SMITH

Wisdom of Silence

We are silent at the beginning of the day because God should have the
first word, and we are silent before going to sleep because
the last word also belongs to God.

DIETRICH BONHOEFFER

I want you woven into a tapestry of love, in touch with everything
there is to know of God. Then you will have minds confident
and at rest, focused on Christ, God's great mystery.
All the richest treasures of wisdom and knowledge
are embedded in that mystery and nowhere else.

COLOSSIANS 2:2-3 MSG

Being able to bow in prayer as the day begins or ends gives expression
to the frustrations and concerns that might not otherwise be ventilated.
On the other end of that prayer line is a loving heavenly Father
who has promised to hear and answer our petitions.

DR. JAMES DOBSON

He calms the storm,
So that its waves are still.
Then they are glad because they are quiet;
So He guides them to their desired haven.

PSALM 107:29–30 NKJV

Sun., Jan. 22, 2023

> Woke up (8:30 P.M.) with this in mind – as a song title – Fix, O Heaven, the Lies By Which We Love

Mon., Jan. 23, 2023

> Thoughts upon waking:

– Hymn: (Title?)

See also
Jesus, Thou
Joy of Loving
Hearts

Oh, Hope of every contrite heart,
O Saviour of mankind,
To those who seek, how kind thou art,
How good to those who find.

– ~~Book Title~~:

Men Who Hate _Women_ ~~and~~ the Women Who Love Them,
Dr. Susan Forward and Joan Torres (New York:
Bantam Books, 1986); from end note in Sandra
Scott's book Charmers and Con Artists & Their Flip Side, no. 4, p. 209.

– Hymn: O God, Our Help in Ages Past (from Ps. 90);
111 in The Hymnbook (Isaac Watts, early 18th Cent.; music
ascribed to William Croft / ST. ANNE : C.M.)

Also, Charlotte Elliott's O Holy Saviour, Friend Unseen
(214 in The Hymnbook); (Friedrich F. Flemming / FLEMMING:
8.8.8.6)

*It is a good discipline to wonder in each new situation
if people wouldn't be better served by our silence than by our words.*

HENRI J. M. NOUWEN

The Music of God

From the heart of God comes the strongest rhythm—
the rhythm of love. Without His love reverberating in us,
whatever we do will come across like a noisy gong or a clanging symbol.
And so the work of the human heart, it seems to me,
is to listen for that music and pick up on its rhythms.

KEN GIRE

Like art, like music, like so many other disciplines, prayer can only be
appreciated when you actually spend time in it. Spending time with
the Master will elevate your thinking. The more you pray, the more
will be revealed. You will appreciate not only the greatness of prayer,
but the greatness of God.

JONI EARECKSON TADA

Life is what we are alive to. It is not length but breadth....
Be alive to...goodness, kindness, purity, love, history, poetry,
music, flowers, stars, God, and eternal hope.

MALTBIE D. BABCOCK

Let God have you, and let God love you—and don't be surprised
if your heart begins to hear music you've never heard and
your feet learn to dance as never before.

MAX LUCADO

Monday, Jan. 23, 2023
> Wake-up hymns: (6 A.M.)
    The Church's One Foundation
    Now I Belong to Jesus
    Make Me a Servant

At the Name of Jesus
There Is a Fountain Filled with Blood
None Other Name

Beyond the sacred page I seek Thee, Lord
(hymn title?)

Mark 5:46
Tues., Jan. 24, 2023
> Hymn: Rejoice, Rejoice, Believers (231 in _The_
    Hymnbook
> Scripture: James 5:8 (from _Daily Light_; vv. 7-11,
    example of Job & compassion and mercy of God;
    Psalm 15, plus Michael F. Ross's exposition in his
    book _The Light of the Psalms_; Hebrews 13:5-6

*S*ing songs to the tune of his glory,
set glory to the rhythms of his praise.

PSALM 66:2 MSG

cf. Malachi 3:16

Hymn 296 in _The Hymnbook_, Come, Ye That Fear the Lord; from Ps. 66; the Psalter, 1912

Time Well Spent

Being present with someone I love is never a waste of time,
especially if God is the one with whom I am present.
Martha complained about Mary wasting time at Jesus' feet
while work piled up.... Indeed, any time spent in prayer seems wasted
to someone who has priorities other than a relationship with God.
For one who loves God, however, there is no more
productive, or necessary, act.

PHILIP YANCEY

Mary...was sitting at Jesus' feet and listening to him teach.
But Martha was busy with all the work to be done. She went in
and said, "Lord, don't you care that my sister has left me alone
to do all the work? Tell her to help me." But the Lord answered her,
"Martha, Martha, you are worried and upset about many things.
Only one thing is important. Mary has chosen the better thing,
and it will never be taken away from her."

LUKE 10:39–42 NCV

Life in the presence of God should be known to us
in conscious experience. It is a life to be enjoyed
every moment of every day.

A. W. TOZER

Tues., 1-24-23

> Point of View author intv. by Kerby Anderson –
Who Lost Afghanistan? by Robert Spencer
His website is JihadWatch.com
George Bush caught up in political correctness;*
 military sidetracked by internal social issues
(*referenced Taliban's Sharia Law emphasis)

Wed., Jan. 25, 2023

> 10 A.M., Wake-up song: ~~Turn~~ Turn Your Eyes
Upon Jesus   (follow-up to initial   his Targeting Tyranny programs)
                        intv. during
> Glen Beck intv. c̄ Amy Nelson (~~Rivet~~ entrepreneur, The Riveter
11 A.M.   lawyer)
 – DOJ & NSA using Amazon's cloud bank   once
 – Hiring hundreds of former CIA and FBI   wrote
   agents   Seattle
                                                         Times
 – Now "allowing" users $5. – pharmacy expense,   articles.
   leading them to give health info. to Amazon
 – Amy's husband Sam was targeted for fraud
   (former Amazon ee; worked to find real estate
   for their expansion across the country). This
   followed Amazon's being sued themselves. Amz.= Jeff Bezos
 – She and her husband fought the charge against him
    and won. She's Emory Univ. alum; earned law degree at (?)

God is never in a hurry but spends years   Has a daughter
  with those He expects to greatly use.   and an "incredible
                                            mother." Father
                                            was suffering incurable
          L. B. COWMAN   disease during Amy's
                                            trial.

Blessings Await

We walk without fear, full of hope and courage and strength
to do His will, waiting for the endless good which He is always giving
as fast as He can get us able to take it in.

GEORGE MACDONALD

God is waiting for us to come to Him with our needs....
God's throne room is always open.... Every single believer
in the whole world could walk into the throne room all at one time,
and it would not even be crowded.

CHARLES STANLEY

The LORD longs to be gracious to you;
he rises to show you compassion.
For the LORD is a God of justice.
Blessed are all who wait for him!

ISAIAH 30:18 NIV

You are never alone. In your heart of hearts, in the place
where no two people are ever alike, Christ is waiting for you.
And what you never dared hope for springs to life.

ROGER OF TAIZÉ

Wed., Jan. 25, 2023
> Hymns: Jesus, Priceless Treasure
    "Man of Sorrows," what a name
    (Hallelujah, What a Saviour!)
Sat., Jan. 28, 2023
> Daily Light (A.M.) - Deut. 33:25; Cf. 33:9
    c̄ Luke 14:26
> Deuteronomy 33:27 - prayer for God to be Judah's
    help against his foes
MONDAY, Jan. 30, 2023
> Luke 1:15c - Note, NIV re: John's filling c̄ Holy
    Spirit "from birth" = Elizabeth's womb
> The Gospel According to Job, Mike Mason:
    - V.I.P., pp. 211-12; Job 19:21
    - Lovelessness, pp. 213-14; Job 19:22
TUESDAY, Jan. 31, 2023
> The Gospel According to Job, Mike Mason
    - Purity of Heart, pp. 345-6; Job 33:8-9
      (sinking 30-ft. putt illus.)

    - Chastening, pp. 347-8; Job 33:19, 29-30
> Daily Light, Bagster/Lotz, Jan. 31, P.M. - Job 33:24

*L*ift up your eyes. Your heavenly Father waits to bless you—
in inconceivable ways to make your life
what you never dreamed it could be.

ANNE ORTLUND

Learning to Listen

Part of our job is simply to be...always attentive to what we are doing
and what is going on inside us, at the same time we listen
and pay attention to the people and events around us. Part of our job
is to expect that, if we are attentive and willing, God will
"give us prayer," will give us the things we need,
"our daily bread," to heal and grow in love.

ROBERTA BONDI

Doing something for you,
bringing something to you—
that's not what you're after.
Being religious, acting pious—
that's not what you're asking for.
You've opened my ears so I can listen.

PSALM 40:6 MSG

If we knew how to listen, we would hear Him speaking to us.
For God does speak.... If we knew how to listen to God, if we knew
how to look around us, our whole life would become prayer.

MICHAEL QUOIST

Jesus is always waiting for us in silence. In that silence,
He will listen to us, there He will speak to our soul,
and there we will hear His voice.

MOTHER TERESA

TUESDAY, Jan. 31, 2023

> Ray Stedman's commentary on Haggai;
<u>Adventuring Through the Bible</u>, pp. 441-449
(Grand Rapids, Michigan: Discovery House
Publishers, 1997 by Elaine Stedman;
Softcover ISBN 1-57293-163-9)

> Job 34:29b, 30 — prayer for national rulers
to be godly lest snares be laid for the people

> <u>The Gospel According to Job</u>, Mike Mason:
  -Free Will, pp. 355-6 (Job 34:33) — Choose
   Christ, choose freedom; Christ, the "railroad
   track"

> BBN's Conference Pulpit:
  Leonard Ravenhill sermon, "How Real Is Your Faith ~~Real~~?"
  Job, Paul, John, Spafford (hymn: It Is Well
  With My Soul), Ravenhill himself (~~broken bones~~
  head to toe following fall from hotel 4th floor),
  "young lady" bedridden (Joni?/offered book
  by a pastor ... she told him she had written it
  herself). Wesley hymn — Thou, O Christ, art all
  I Want

*T*he more faithfully you listen to the voice within you,
the better you will hear what is sounding outside.

DAG HAMMARSKJÖLD

Nature's Silent Beauty

Experience God in the breathless wonder and startling beauty
that is all around you. His sun shines warm upon your face.
His wind whispers in the treetops. Like the first rays of morning light,
celebrate the start of each day with God.

WENDY MOORE

God is here! I hear His voice
While thrushes make the woods rejoice.
I touch His robe each time I place
My hand against a pansy's face.
I breathe His breath if I but pass
Verbenas trailing through the grass.
God is here! From every tree
His leafy fingers beckon me.

MADELEINE AARON

Silently one by one, in the
infinite meadow of heaven
blossomed the lovely stars,
the forget-me-nots of the angels.

HENRY WADSWORTH LONGFELLOW

Tuesday, Feb. 7, 2023

> <u>My Utmost for His Highest</u>, Oswald Chambers :
"The Discipline of Dejection" — my responsibility
to not be dejected. E.g., "answered" prayer
not an issue — union c̄ God is

Sat., Mar. 4, 2023

> <u>Look Unto Me : The Devotions of Charles
Spurgeon</u>; James G. Reimann, Ed.; 2008;
(Grand Rapids, Michigan : Zondervan; ISBN
978-0-310-28387-4) : June 10 (Day 162 —
Romans 14:8; Horatius Bonar verse based
on Song 2:10 KJV; Sept. 30 (Day 274 —
Ps. 66:2; Francis Xavier (1506-1552) verse,
(Hymn: My God, I Love Thee)(?)

Wed., 3/09/2023 (12:02 A.m)

> Hymn : O God, Our Help in Ages Past (Watts/Croft) —
Two five-verse versions, having each a different
Verse 4; Option 1 :
   Time, like an ever-rolling stream, Bears all its sons away;
   They fly, forgotten, as a dream Dies at the opening day.
   (No. 11, <u>Crowning Glory Hymnal</u> — Singspiration, Inc.,
1964)

O LORD, what a variety of things you have made!
In wisdom you have made them all. The earth is full of your creatures.

PSALM 104:24 NLT

For Himself

Although it is good to think upon the kindness of God,
and to love Him and worship Him for it, it is far better
to gaze upon the pure essence of Him and to love Him
and worship Him for Himself.

Stand up and praise the LORD your God.... You alone are the LORD.
You made the heavens, even the highest heavens,
and all their starry host, the earth and all that is on it,
the seas and all that is in them. You give life to everything,
and the multitudes of heaven worship you.

NEHEMIAH 9:5–6 NIV

We desire many things, and God offers us only one thing.
He can offer us only one thing—Himself. He has nothing else to give.
There is nothing else to give.

PETER KREEFT

The reason for loving God is God Himself,
and the measure in which we should love Him
is to love Him without measure.

BERNARD OF CLAIRVAUX

3/09/23 (cont.)

> Hymn: O God, Our Help in Ages Past (Watts/Croft)
  -Verse 4, Option 2:
  A thousand ages, in Thy sight, Are like an evening gone;
  Short as the watch that ends the night, Before the
      rising sun.   (No. 8, Worship and Service Hymnal)

In all cases, four identical verses, with first and
final verses using exactly the same words:

1) O God, our Help in ...
2) Under the shadow ...
3) Before the hills ...
4) O God, our Help in ...

> Two following hymns from Worship and Service
  Hymnal -
    No. 9, When All Thy Mercies, O My God
    No. 10, Praise Ye the Lord, the Almighty

*J*oy is perfect acquiesce in God's will because
the soul delights itself in God Himself.

H. W. WEBB-PEPLOE

Seek His Face

The person who asks for and seeks this one thing from the Lord
makes his petition confidently and serenely. This is the one,
true and only life of happiness that...we should contemplate
the Lord's graciousness forever.

AUGUSTINE

I have been away and come back again many times to this place.
Each time I approach, I regret ever having left. There is a peace here,
a serenity, even before I enter. Just the idea of returning becomes
a balm for the wounds I've collected elsewhere. Before I can finish
even one knock, the door opens wide and I am in His presence.

BARBARA FARMER

As we practice the presence of God, more and more we find ourselves
going through the stresses and strains of daily activity with an ease
and serenity that amazes even us...especially us.

RICHARD J. FOSTER

The serene beauty of a holy life
is the most powerful influence in the world
next to the power of God.

BLAISE PASCAL

Friday, March 11, 2023
> In _The Gospel According to Job_ (Mike Mason):
- Mercy, pp. 179-80 (Job 16:4-5) / Romans exposition;
  Shakespeare quote
- Resurrection, pp. 163-64 (Job 14:14)
> _Desiring God_ (John Piper): (chapter title, "Conversion")
  Page 59, note 3 - George MacDonald quote re: hell
  as remedial. Two books referenced - _Creation_
  in Christ, ed. Rolland Hein (Wheaton, Ill.: Harold
  Shaw, 1976); cites MacDonald's sermon "Justice."
  Second book, _The J. I. Packer Collection_,
  ℰ selected and introduced by Alister McGrath
  (Downers Grove, Ill.: InterVarsity, 2000), 210-26.
> _Taste and See_ (John Piper):
- Meditation 68: "Lord of the Dead," references two verses
  also cited in Mason's book under Resurrection
  (see above) - Isa. 26:19; Daniel 12:2
- Meditation 94: "Martin Luther's Rules for How to
  Become a Theologian," focus on Ps. 119 -
  1) prayer, 2) meditation, 3) trials. Includes
  quotes from Ewald M. Plass, compiler, _What Luther_
  Says: An Anthology [St. Louis: Concordia Publishing
                    House, 1959], v. 3, 1359f.

Give thanks to the LORD, call on his name;
Look to the LORD and his strength; seek his face always.

PSALM 105:1, 4 NIV

His Quiet Care

Try to find a quiet place. Outward silence develops inward silence;
and outward silence improves inward silence as it begins
to take root in your life.

MADAME GUYON

Be still, and in the quiet moments, listen to the voice
of your heavenly Father. His words can renew your spirit...
no one knows you and your needs like He does.

JANET L. WEAVER SMITH

I'm asking GOD for one thing, only one thing:
To live with him in his house my whole life long.
I'll contemplate his beauty;
I'll study at his feet.
That's the only quiet, secure place in a noisy world,
The perfect getaway.

PSALM 27:4–5 MSG

Ask God to help you truly know Him as the Great I AM.
Ask Him to help you lay aside your *to-do* list while you spend
quality quiet time getting to know Him. This way, you can
learn to *be* with Him in everything you *do*.

AMY AND JUDGE REINHOLD

Wed., 3-15-23

> The New Exhaustive of the Bible
  Strong's Concordance : (Nashville, Tennessee: Thomas Nelson, Inc., Publishers; 1990)

  Greek dictionary, p. 98 - no. 5503. Χήρα
  chēra (khay'-rah) - from 5490, chasma
  (khas'-mah) meaning chasm or gape; 5503
  figurative meaning is widow.

Friday, 3-17-2023
> Two hymns by John Bowring :
  1) God Is Love, His Mercy Brightens
  2) In the Cross of Christ

Wed., 3/29/2023
> Hymns based on the tune St. Flavian : C.M.;
  Day's Psalter, 1563 :
  1) My Soul with Expectation (from Psalm 62;
     Scottish Psalter, 1650) - 113 in The Hymnbook
  2) Lord, Who Throughout These Forty Days
     (Claudia F. Hernaman, 1873) - 181, The Hymnbook
  3) Be Known to Us in Breaking Bread (James Montgomery,
     1825) - 446, The Hymnbook

The miracle comes quietly into the mind
that stops an instant and is still.

R. FISHEL

God's Eternal Love

The LORD is like a father to his children,
tender and compassionate to those who fear him.
For he knows how weak we are;
he remembers we are only dust.
Our days on earth are like grass;
like wildflowers, we bloom and die.
The wind blows, and we are gone—
as though we had never been here.
But the love of the LORD remains forever....
The LORD has made the heavens his throne;
from there he rules over everything.

PSALM 103:13–17, 19 NLT

The reason we can dare to risk loving others is that
"God has for Christ's sake loved us." Think of it! We are loved eternally,
totally, individually, unreservedly! Nothing can take God's love away.

GLORIA GAITHER

Great is his love toward us,
and the faithfulness of the LORD endures forever.

PSALM 117:2 NIV

I am wholly His; I am peculiarly His;
I am universally His; I am eternally His.

THOMAS BENTON BROOKS

Thursday, March 30, 2023
> A.M. hymns:
- Come We that Love the Lord
- I Want a Principle Within (& Faith Is the Victory!)
- Love Divine, All Loves Excelling
- Spirit of God, Descend Upon My Heart
- Throned Upon the Awful Tree (197 in
    The Hymnbook); John Ellerton, 1875;
    ARFON: 7.7.7.7.7.7, Welsh Hymn Melody,
    Har. by Hugh Davies
> Scripture, early A.M.: 1 Cor. 15:19
Sat., April 1, 2023
> Scripture (early A.M.) - James 2:19 / entire passage =
vv. 14-26; Luke 6:46 (see also vv. 47-49)
> Hymn - Day by Day
    (Others: cont. memorization ~~of stanzas 2(&3)~~ I Want
    A Principle Within; Trust and Obey; Jesus
    ~~The~~ Loves Even Me, by P.P. Bliss - words & music;
    The Lily of the Valley, or I've Found a Friend in
    Jesus)

*Amid the ebb and flow of the passing world,
our God remains unmoved, and His throne endures forever.*

ROBERT COLEMAN

Silent Reverence

A spiritual discipline...is the concentrated effort to create some
inner and outer space in our lives, where...obedience can be practiced.
Through a spiritual discipline we prevent the world from
filling our lives to such an extent that there is no place left to listen.
A spiritual discipline sets us free to pray or, to say it better,
allows the Spirit of God to pray in us.

HENRI J. M. NOUWEN

There are times when to speak is to violate the moment...
when silence represents the highest respect. The word for such times
is reverence. The prayer for such times is "Hallowed be thy name."

MAX LUCADO

Over the margins of life comes a whisper, a faint call,
a premonition of richer living which we know we are passing by.
Strained by the very mad pace of our daily outer burdens,
we are further strained by an inward uneasiness, because we have
hints that there is a way of life vastly richer and deeper than
all this hurried existence, a life of unhurried serenity
and peace and power.

THOMAS R. KELLY

Tues., 4-18-23

"What makes a Christian a Christian is not perfection but forgiveness." (2 Cor. 5:21)
— Max Lucado; from _Walking with the Savior_

"It is a positive crime to be weak in God's strength."
— Oswald Chambers; from _My Utmost for His Highest_, April 14th ("Inspired Invicibility;" Matthew 11:29)

Turning Points, Dr. David Jeremiah — "Every Day," April 18 (p. 113): Ps. 139:16/NLT. [Mentions Elvis Presley's interest in Eastern religions/spiritual matters which he discussed with his hairdresser, Larry Geller.] "God has a life purpose for us." Seek to find it and do it daily, at his direction. (Presley was wanting to know why he was who he was — how did he get to be "Elvis.")

The LORD is in his holy temple;
let all the earth be silent before him.

HABAKKUK 2:20 NIV

Windows of Our Soul

Open wide the windows of our spirits and fill us full of light;
open wide the door of our hearts that we may receive and entertain
Thee with all the powers of our adoration.

CHRISTINA ROSSETTI

Live for today but hold your hands open to tomorrow.
Anticipate the future and its changes with joy. There is a seed
of God's love in every event, every circumstance, every...
situation in which you may find yourself.

BARBARA JOHNSON

Let my soul be at rest again, for the Lord has been good to me....
And so I walk in the LORD's presence as I live here on earth!

PSALM 116:7, 9 NLT

Day-to-day living becomes a window through which we get a glimpse
of life eternal. The eternal illuminates and gives focus to the daily.

JANICE RIGGLE HUIE

To know ourselves loved
Is to have the
Depths of our own
Capacity to love
Opened up.

J. MAIN

Sat., May 19, 2023
- Daily Light, A.M. : 1 Tim. 4:16, 17 and others, incl. Eph. 6. Ministerial calling.
- ~~Faith's Checkbook~~ (Spurgeon) – Isa. 45: ~~I~~ – "We Dare Not Doubt" God with Joshua as he was with Moses
- The Valley of Vision :
    Cry for Deliverance, pp. 168-9
    Sincerity, pp. 316-17
    Joy, pp. 292-3

Tuesday, May 23, 2023
> Spurgeon's Faith's Checkbook : (Ps. 72:12; "Full Reliance on God")
> Oswald Chambers' My Utmost for His Highest : "Careful [care-full] Infidelity" (rather than loyal abandonment to God); Matthew 6:25

Friday, June 9, 2023
> Wake-up ~~song~~ : His love will not take (me) you
    (refrain?)   where his grace cannot keep (me) you,
                And when you are faltering, (I am)
                he still will see you through. (me)
                (his grace)

*J*ust as there comes a warm sunbeam into every cottage window,
so comes a love—born of God's care for every separate need.

NATHANIEL HAWTHORNE

Alone with God

There is no true, deep conversion, no true, deep holiness,
no clothing with the Holy Spirit and with power, no abiding peace
or joy, without being daily alone with God. What an inestimable
privilege is the institution of daily secret prayer to begin every morning.
Let it be one thing that our hearts are set on.

ANDREW MURRAY

It is not objective proof of God's existence that we want but the
experience of God's presence. That is the miracle we are really after,
and that is also, I think, the miracle that we really get.

FREDERICK BUECHNER

God loves to look at us, and loves it when we will look back at Him.
Even when we try to run away from our troubles...God will find us,
bless us, even when we feel most alone, unsure.... God will find a way
to let us know that He is with us *in this place*, wherever we are.

KATHLEEN NORRIS

The Spirit of prayer makes us so intimate with God that we scarcely
pass through an experience before we speak to Him about it.

OLE HALLESBY

Wed., 6-14-23
> The Valley of Vision:
Christian Calling (p. 90); Continual Repentance
(p. 136); Voyage (p. 202); Comforts (p. 300),
also today's A.M. Daily Light topic (comfort in
suffering)
> Edges of His Ways, A. Carmichael - June 25:
Eph. 5:19. "God make us a singing company."
> John Piper's Taste and See:
No. 40 - The Root of Mental Health (not "self-"
worth, but God), pp. 124-6
No. 21 - How to Be Filled with the Holy Spirit
(Eph. 5:18-21) - "drink and pray" the apostolic
teachings and Christ's words. Eph. 3:19 esp.
(4-)
> I Corinthians 13:5 - Love... does not act unbecomingly;
it does not seek its own, is not provoked, does not take
into account a wrong (suffered)... (v.6ff)
> Tabletalk (Ligonier Ministries, 421 Ligonier Court,
Sanford, FL 32771), June 2017. Cover painting: Christ
Healing the Paralytic at the Pool of Bethesda, Bartolome
Esteban Murillo, Seventeenth Century.

He alone is my rock and my salvation....
Pour out your hearts to him, for God is our refuge.

PSALM 62:6, 8 NLT

The Spiritual Life

The spiritual life is first of all a life. It is not merely something to be
known and studied, it is to be lived.... We live as spiritual people when
we live as people seeking God. If we are to become spiritual,
we must remain human.

THOMAS MERTON

I stayed awake all night,
prayerfully pondering your promise....
You're the closest of all to me, GOD,
and all your judgments true.

PSALM 119:148, 151 MSG

Prayer is the way the life of God is nourished. Our ordinary views
of prayer are not found in the New Testament. We look upon prayer
as a means of getting things for ourselves; the Bible's idea of prayer
is that we may get to know God Himself.

OSWALD CHAMBERS

Prayer is by nature a dialogue between man and God.
It unites the soul with its Creator and reconciles the two.
Its effect is to hold the world together.

JOHN OF THE LADDER

Wed., 6-14-23

> Tabletalk Daily Bible Studies : Into the Word,
June 2017 - Faith Alone; Wednesday, June 14 -
Justification and Sin : Romans 4:6-8, 1-5; 5:12-21;
I Cor. 1:30; II Cor. 5:21. Further study : Psalm 130:3-4;
Isaiah 55:6-7; Micah 7:18-20; I John 2:12.
See also R.C. Sproul's book, Faith Alone. Not
Christ plus works, not baptism plus penance per
Roman Catholic teaching. Faith alone, including
non-imputation of sin -- sin not held against us,
even though we still sin.

> My Utmost for His Highest, Oswald Chambers -
June 14th; Get a Move On : In the Matter of
Determination, John 15:4. "God will not make me
think like Jesus, I have to do it myself; I have to bring
every thought into captivity to the obedience of Christ."
(2 Cor. 10:5) "Determine to abide in Jesus wherever
you are placed." "... not a bandbox life" (Indexed under
NOW, p. 274)
Hymn : Constantly Abiding (Mrs. Will L. Murphy)
d. 1942

The highest pinnacle of the spiritual life is not joy in unbroken sunshine,
but absolute and undoubting trust in the love of God.

A. W. THOROLD

1 Peter 5:7
Romans 8:28

Guided by His Hand

To You, O Lord, I lift up my soul.
O my God, in You I trust....
Make me know Your ways, O Lord;
teach me Your paths.
Lead me in Your truth and teach me,
for You are the God of my salvation;
for You I wait all the day.
Remember, O Lord, Your compassion
and Your lovingkindnesses,
for they have been from of old.

Psalm 25:1–2, 4–6 nasb

We are of such value to God that He came to live among us...
and to guide us home. He will go to any length to seek us,
even to being lifted high upon the cross to draw us back to Himself.
We can only respond by loving God for His love.

Catherine of Sienna

God guides us.... He leads us step by step, from event to event.
Only afterwards...do we experience the feeling of having been led
without knowing it, the feeling that God has mysteriously guided us.

Paul Tournier

You guide me with your counsel,
leading me to a glorious destiny.

Psalm 73:24 nlt

Wed., 6-14-23

> Voices of the Saints, Bert Ghezzi

(50) Bridget of Sweden (1303-1373; d. 7-23-1373),
pages 100-101. Rebuked royal court at Naples after
pilgrimage to Jerusalem in 1371 about their
physical immorality (incl. abortion) and spiritual
adultery. Prophetic like Jeremiah. Established
Brigittines religious order where she tended to
("ruled over" as abbess) temporal affairs, and the
men over spiritual matters. This was after she became
Ulf Gudmarsson's widow (he a landowner; married 28
yrs. c̄ 8 children); she chose thereafter to live a
celibate and austere life.

(276) Olaf (995-1030), pages 552-3. Violent pirate
who on his own took the kingship of Norway (became
its king). Forceful evangelist. Routed by landowners
with help of King Canute of England and Denmark.
One year later was killed in battle to regain kingship.

The Lord is able to guide. The promises cover
every imaginable situation.... Take the hand He stretches out.

ELISABETH ELLIOT

Expressions of Nature

Sunshine spills through autumn-colored leaves, lighting up
their brilliance like stained-glass windows in a great cathedral,
expressing the wonder of God's love, declaring His glory.

If you have never heard the mountains singing, or seen the trees of the
field clapping their hands, do not think because of that they don't.
Ask God to open your ears so you may hear it, and your eyes
so you may see it, because, though few people ever know it,
they do, my friend, they do.

MCCANDLISH PHILLIPS

I see in the stars, in the rivers, I see in the open fields, patches of heaven
and threads of paradise. Let me sew the earth, the day, the way
of my life into a pattern that forms a quilt, God's quilt,
to keep me warm today and always.

CHRISTOPHER DE VINCK

The sunshine dancing on the water, the lulling sound of waves
rolling into the shore, the glittering stars against the night sky—
all God's light, His warmth, His majesty—our Father of light
reaching out to us, drawing each of us closer to Himself.

WENDY MOORE

Wed., June 14, 2023 (Flag Day)

> Reviewed a few index entries in David McCullough's
1776*: (centered on battle for Long Island, NY) ⤸
- patriotism, 3, 159, 226, 251   ⤷ just so happened...
                                       not specifically chosen
- Reed, Joseph, 44, 66 (Philadelphia lawyer)/(London-trained)
   character and personality of, 201, 204-5 "general orders"
Pg. 159 incl. quote of Gen. Washington's ~~address~~ to
   soldiers, appealing to their pride, patriotism, & love of liberty.
Pg. 204 incl. sentence from Reed to his wife
   Esther: "We think (at least I do) that we cannot
   stay, ~~Joseph Reed wrote~~ and yet we do not know
   how to go, so that we may be properly said to be
   between hawk and buzzard."
(My sentiments exactly !!)
- Also Lee, Richard Henry (Va. congressman), 41, 255
   Pg. 41 has quote of his ~~feelings~~ thoughts about Yankees
   ("exceeding dirty and nasty")
   Pg. 255 mentions Reed and Lee as to their
   loyalty to Washington

* ISBN-13: 978-0-7432-2671-4
   ISBN-10: 0-7432-2671-2
   Simon & Schuster (2005)

*Y*ou will go out in joy and be led forth in peace;
the mountains and hills will burst into song before you,
and all the trees of the field will clap their hands.

ISAIAH 55:12 NIV

Listening Prayer

Lord, teach me to listen. The times are noisy and my ears are weary
with the thousand raucous sounds which continuously assault them...
let me hear You speaking in my heart. Let me get used to the sound
of Your voice, that its tones may be familiar when the sounds
of the earth die away and the only sound will be the music
of Your speaking voice. Amen.

A. W. TOZER

If we do not listen we do not come to the truth. If we do not pray
we do not even get as far as listening.... Four things go together:
silence, listening, prayer, truth.

HUBERT VAN ZELLER

Prayer is not asking. Prayer is putting oneself in the hands of God,
at His disposition, and listening to His voice
in the depths of our hearts.

MOTHER TERESA

God is not interested in you praying perfectly;
He just wants to spend time with you and be able
to speak with you and know you are listening.

DR. HENRY CLOUD

Thursday, 6-15-2023

> The Valley of Vision
   The Divine Will, p.14; Divine Support, p.212;
   Divine Promises, p.240; Divine Mercies, p.216

> Eph. 5:15 - 21; J. B. Phillips heading:
   You know the truth -> let your life show it!
   Live life, then, with a due sense of responsibility,
   ... thank God the Father at all times for
   everything, in the name of our Lord Jesus Christ.
   ...   (See Page 407.)

   J. B. Phillips
   the New Testament in Modern English
   Student Edition / Revised Edition
   Macmillan Publishing Company
   New York
   ISBN 0-02-088570-9
   First Paperback Edition 1972

> Anxious for Nothing, John MacArthur (Grace To You host)
                                    (1993)   GTY.org
2006 Rev. ed. of Anxiety Attacked - Victor Books, an imprint of
                                Cook Communications Ministries -
   Pp. 160-1 of Appendix: Psalms for the Anxious: Colorado
            (NIV)   (NIV)   Sprgs. CO;
   Ps. 90: 13-15, 17ₐ; 91: 1-2, 14-15ₐ; 100: 2,5 (KJV); Paris;
   and page 166; Psalm 142: 1-3 (TLB)   Ontario;
                                                    Kingsway
                                                    Communications,
   I listen carefully to what God the Lᴏʀᴅ is saying, Eastbourn
      for he speaks peace to his faithful people.   Eastbourne,
                                                    England

         Pꜱᴀʟᴍ 85:8 ɴʟᴛ

Stillness of Creation

✔   In the forest we can learn life's lessons if we will—
How to turn towards the sunshine, standing straight and still,
How to be content with slow development and grow
In grace and strength in spite of storms, of wind and frost and snow.

PATIENCE STRONG

In the beginning God created the heavens and the earth....
Then God saw everything that He had made,
and indeed it was very good.... On the seventh day God ended His work
which He had done, and He rested.... Then God blessed the seventh day
and sanctified it, because in it He rested from all His work.

GENESIS 1:1, 31; 2:2–3 NKJV   xoxo

✔   Nothing in all creation is so like God as stillness.

MEISTER ECKHART

Living becomes an awesome business when you realize
that you spend every moment of your life in the sight
and company of an omniscient, omnipresent Creator.

J. I. PACKER

The day is done, the sun has set,
Yet light still tints the sky;
My heart stands still
In reverence,
For God is passing by.

RUTH ALLA WAGER

Friday, 6-16-23

None But Jesus, John Flavel (Banner of Truth
   Pocket Puritans) — p. 138 — nos. 328, 329, 330 :
   quotes from Assembly's Catechism and The
   Reasonableness of Personal Reformation
   on joy, troubles, melancholy; good man
   vs. wicked man as to how each regards
   the other

This could be the day (that the Lord returns in glory!)
(part of a song)

Christ Church Press, "The Pastor's Pen" (GKR):
> January 2006 — Jeremiah 33:3,9 — pray
   that you may be "a joy, a praise, and an honor
   to God."
> June 2007 — Isaiah 54:2 — on moving to new
   sanctuary May 13th (Mother's Day). "Driven stakes" =
   understanding increased thru good doctrine; result,
   "spread / stretched out curtains" = reaching the lost,
   "an enduring harvest." (GKR)

*Nature has been for me, for as long as I can remember,
a source of solace, inspiration, adventure, and delight.*

LORRAINE ANDERSON

Jesus, Lover of My Soul

Solitude is a place inside myself where God's Spirit and my spirit dwell together in union. This place within me is private and reserved for the intimacies that God and I share. What happens between the two of us in that place is not meant for public consumption. It is a place where I can give myself with abandon to the Lover of my soul.

RUTH HALEY BARTON

If you are seeking after God, you may be sure of this:
God is seeking you much more. He is the Lover,
and you are His beloved. He has promised Himself to you.

JOHN OF THE CROSS

Time passed in silence with God is time spent growing in relationship with Him. And time spent letting His love flow through you to others is an investment in eternity.

AMY AND JUDGE REINHOLD

You are in the Beloved...therefore infinitely
dear to the Father, unspeakably precious to Him.
You are never, not for one second, alone.

NORMAN DOWTY

Friday, 6-16-23

> Christ Church Press, "the Pastor's Pen" (GRR):

- July 2005: Final paragraph defines "good preaching" as prepared hearers (both speaker(s) and listeners) who eagerly respond to God's word with demonstrable obedience.

- July 2006: Mentions "that old Gospel song" "I Need Jesus"; Matt. 11:28; overcoming temptations and trials; daily decisions/responsibilities; prayer and meditation. Begins with (and ends with) ref. to "sermon title posted on a church bulletin board," "Come Apart or Go to Pieces." (I'm reminded how he once shared in a sermon that one of his former congregation members said, "We don't need 'Gordon Reed' anymore." (A favorable state of affairs, that... they'd been prepared thru good teaching/preaching for his departure.) As always, Psalm 118:8 — It is better to take refuge in the LORD than to trust in man. Thank you, God, for Gordon Reed. Said from the heart, though some hesitation afterward

- Wilmer Wallace's Art Showing — June 2010: follow-up report with photos, July 2010. Sorry didn't go and take Mom (or others?) along. Mentioned his having gone thru a "dark and difficult time." Likely Jo's (Georleen's) death; not sure that's all, though.

The LORD is righteous in all his ways and loving toward all he has made. The LORD is near to all who call on him, to all who call on him in truth.

PSALM 145:17–18 NIV

Grace for the Moment, Max Lucado
"Needed: One Great Saviour" (June 16)
Romans 3:23-24 / Paul; Peter ~~~~~~~~~~~

His Dwelling Place

In Solomon's day God dwelt in a temple made of stone;
today He dwells in a temple composed of living believers.
When we really see that God has made our hearts His dwelling place,
what a deep reverence will come over our lives!

WATCHMAN NEE

Imagine yourself as a living house. God comes in to rebuild that house....
You thought you were going to be made into a decent little cottage:
but He is building a palace. He intends to come and live in it Himself.

C. S. LEWIS

You are living stones that God is building into his spiritual temple.
What's more, you are his holy priests.

1 PETER 2:5 NLT

The soul is a temple, and God is silently building it by night and by day.
Precious thoughts are building it; unselfish love is building it;
all-penetrating faith is building it.

HENRY WARD BEECHER

We cannot kindle when we will
The fire that in the heart resides
The spirit bloweth and is still
In mystery our soul abides.

MATTHEW ARNOLD

Sunday, June 18, 2023   (69 in _The Hymnbook_)

> A.M. Hymns: "This Is the Day" (Isaac Watts -
   Ps. 118); "Whiter than Snow" (James Nicholson /
   Wm. G. Fischer - late 19th century)

> Faith's Checkbook, C.H. Spurgeon - June 18
   "God Himself Shall Work"
   Isaiah 33:10 (and Ps. 57; my addition)
   Hymn brought to mind:
                                    Joseph Swain
   "O Thou, in Whose Presence" (~~John G. Whittier~~ /
   ~~Aaron~~ Freeman Lewis - late 18th century); 370
   in _Worship and Service Hymnal_ - Tune, MEDITATION

> Other hymns from same hymnal:
   369 "The Great Physician" (Wm. Hunter / John H. Stockton,
                                              late 19th c.)
   371 "I Know Not What the Future Hath"
         (J.G. Whittier / A.J. Abbey, late 19th c.)

> From _The Hymnbook_:
   70 "O Day of Rest and Gladness" (Christopher Wordsworth /
      Old German melody; Arr. by Lowell Mason, 1839)

_If_ each moment is sacred—
a time and place where we encounter God—
life itself is sacred.

JEAN M. BLOMQUIST
He Is There and He Is Not Silent, Francis Schaeffer

Taste and See

If we begin to worship and come to God again and again
by meditating, by reading, by prayer, and by obedience, little by little
God becomes known to us through experience. We enter into a sweet
familiarity with God, and by tasting how sweet the Lord is
we pass into...loving God, not for our own sake, but for Himself.

BERNARD OF CLAIRVAUX

All [God's] glory and beauty come from within, and there He
delights to dwell. His visits there are frequent, His conversation sweet,
His comforts refreshing, His peace passing all understanding.

THOMAS À KEMPIS

I come to the garden alone
while the dew is still on the roses,
And the voice I hear, falling on my ear,
the Son of God discloses.

He speaks, and the sound of His voice
is so sweet the birds hush their singing.
And the melody that He gave to me
within my heart is ringing.

And He walks with me, and He talks with me,
and He tells me I am his own.
And the joy we share as we tarry there
none other has ever known.

C. AUSTIN MILES

Sat., 7-15-23
Job 30:31; 31:15; 31:23; 33:6-7; 37:19-24;
     38:1; 40:6; 41:11
Sat., 7-22-23
Hebrews 9:15; 6:19; 12:14; 3:1; 7:23-28 (esp. 7:25)
Matt. 10:16, 23
Sunday, 7-23-23
Oswald Chambers on sanctification, in My
Utmost for His Highest: July 22 & 23: it
is impartation, not imitation, involving
the death of me to all else (others & what
they think of me) and the receiving of
Christ as my life, my all. Results
include sanity.
Friday, July 28, 2023
Pss. 7:11; 12:8; 16:3 (note alt. trnsl. in NIV-84 note), 4.
Ps. 19:12

Open your mouth and taste, open your eyes and see—how good GOD is.
Blessed are you who run to him.

PSALM 34:8 MSG

In Silent Strength

A living, loving God can and does make His presence felt,
can and does speak to us in the silence of our hearts, can and does warm
and caress us till we no longer doubt that He is near, that He is here.

BRENNAN MANNING

The sound of "gentle stillness" after all the thunder and wind have
passed will be the ultimate Word from God.

JIM ELLIOT

The wonder of living is held within the beauty of silence, the glory
of sunlight...the sweetness of fresh spring air, the quiet strength of earth,
and the love that lies at the very root of all things.

God walks with us.... He scoops us up in His arms or simply sits with us
in silent strength until we cannot avoid the awesome recognition
that yes, even now, He is here.

GLORIA GAITHER

Open my eyes that I may see
Glimpses of truth Thou hast for me.
Place in my hands the wonderful key
That shall unclasp and set me free:
Silently now I wait for Thee,
Ready, my God, Thy will to see;
Open my eyes, illumine me, Spirit divine!

CLARA H. SCOTT

Sunday, 7-30-2023
> Bible reading: Pss. 25:15; 26:8; 27:6c; 28:7c;
Pss. 30:12a (& vs. 11); 31:9-10; 32:10-11;
Ps. 33 (entire Psalm, 22 vss.) (God as creator
and supreme authority, worthy of trust, keeper
of his own people); Pss. 34 (all 22 vss.);
35:15-17; 36:11

Monday, July 31, 2023
> Taste and See, John Piper:
• "Ten Reasons to Love the Truth" (No. 31 -
   pp. 101-4); 2 Thess. 2:10, et al.
  Starts with Michael Novak quote from
  May 5, 1994 address at Westminster Abbey
  (from First Things, No. 45, August/September
  1994).
• "If You Believe, You Will See the Glory of
  God," John 11:14-15, 40. Note the two
  different responses to Lazarus's being
  raised from the dead. ¶ at end (final
  paragraph = good prayer (pp. 182-3).

Rest in the Lord

Rest is not idleness, and to lie sometimes on the grass under the trees
on a summer's day, listening to the murmur of water, or watching
the clouds float across the sky, is by no means a waste of time.

SIR JOHN LUBBOCK

God provides resting places as well as working places. Rest, then,
and be thankful when He brings you, wearied, to a wayside well.

L. B. COWMAN

True silence is the rest of the mind; it is to the spirit
what sleep is to the body: nourishment and refreshment.

WILLIAM PENN

Relax, everything's going to be all right;
rest, everything's coming together;
open your hearts, love is on the way!

JUDE 1:2 MSG   *Wow!*

Joy comes from knowing God loves me and knows who I am
and where I'm going...that my future is secure as I rest in Him.

DR. JAMES DOBSON

Monday, July 31, 2023
> Taste and See, John Piper:
  • "Take Heed How You Hear!" (No. 115-
    pp. 140-143); Luke 8:18. Preparing
  for Sunday worship; ten items,
  from heart preparation by prayer to
  desiring truth above riches and food
  (Ps. 19:10-11).
Tuesday, August 1, 2023
> Ps. 40:11, 12, 17b; Ps. 44:21b
  John 1:34
Wed., Sept. 2, 2023
> 1 Timothy 4:10c; I Cor. 2:6c
  Friday, 8-04-23
> Ps. 42:8; Ps. 46:12-13; Ps. 50:22-23
  John 2:11, 25
  Sunday, 8-13-23: Ahead in "Joy in His Presence"
  section (oops!); also Bert Ghezzi, Voices of the
  Saints: Mary of the Angels and Cuthbert, "Wonder
  Worker of Britain."

Peace Be Still

Peace is not placidity: peace is
The power to endure the megatron of pain
With joy, the silent thunder of release,
The ordering of Love. Peace is the atom's start,
The primal image: God within the heart.

MADELEINE L'ENGLE

Peace I leave with you, My peace I give to you; not as the world gives
do I give to you. Let not your heart be troubled, neither let it be afraid.

JOHN 14:27 NKJV

Calm me O Lord as you stilled the storm,
Still me O Lord, keep me from harm.
Let all the tumult within me cease,
Enfold me, Lord, in Your peace.

CELTIC TRADITIONAL

Unceasing Prayer has a way of speaking peace to the chaos.
Our fractured and fragmented activities begin focusing
around a new Center of Reference. We experience peace,
stillness, serenity, firmness of life orientation.

RICHARD J. FOSTER

The time, how lonely and how still
Peace shines and smiles on all below
The plain, the stream, the wood, the hill
All fair with evening's setting glow.

AMISH HYMN

Sunday, 8-13-23

> Proverbs :

Ch.	No. of Verses (Total)		
1 -	33	27 -	27
2 -	22	28 -	28
3 -	35	29 -	27
4 -	27	30 -	33
5 -	23	31 -	31
6 -	35		
7 -	27		
8 -	36		
9 -	18		
10 -	32		
11 -	31		
12 -	28		
13 -	25		
14 -	35		
15 -	33		
16 -	33		
17 -	28		
18 -	24		
19 -	29		
20 -	30		
21 -	31		
22 -	29		
23 -	35		
24 -	34		
25 -	28		
26 -	28		

Christ is the still point of the turning world.

T. S. ELIOT

Open Your Heart

The "air" which our souls need also envelops all of us at all times
and on all sides. God is round about us in Christ on every hand,
with many-sided and all-sufficient grace.
All we need to do is to open our hearts.

OLE HALLESBY

Jesus Christ opens wide the doors of the treasure house
of God's promises, and bids us go in and take with boldness
the riches that are ours.

CORRIE TEN BOOM

Life begins each morning.... Each morning is the open door
to a new world—new vistas, new aims, new tryings.

LEIGH MITCHELL HODGES

The steadfast love of the Lord never ceases, his mercies never come
to an end; they are new every morning; great is your faithfulness.

LAMENTATIONS 3:22–23 NRSV

I can drink freely of God's power and experience His
touch of refreshment and blessing—much like
an invigorating early spring rain.

ANABEL GILLHAM

~~Sunday~~
Monday, 8-1~~4~~-23

> A.M. hymns: (in <u>The Hymnbook</u>)

438 - Within Thy Temple's Sacred Courts (Ps. 48)

436 - City of God

243 - Spirit Divine, Attend Our Prayers (alt. tune for 436)

270 - Lord Jesus, Think on Me

267 - Jesus Is Tenderly Calling Thee Home

Monday, 8-14-23

> Scripture reading: Prov. 14 ; Pss. 71, 72; Mark 4:1-

6:20. Verses of interest: Ps. 71:7, 12; Mark 4:40;

5:41 ; 6:3, 17   No transfiguration here: } ... "took him along, (4:35-41)
Nothing extraordinary   "just as he was"
... " who is this ? "
— they thought they were in control, but really he was!
and is !!

(always is. whew;
thank you, Jesus,
thank you, God.

Sunday, Aug. 20, 2023

> P.M. hymns, from <u>Worship and Service Hymnal</u>:

Nos. 87, 88, 219: ~~What~~ What if It Were Today?;
The King Shall Come When Morning Dawns;
When I See the Blood / (Christ our Redeemer
died on the cross)

Faith goes up the stairs that love has made
and looks out the window which hope has opened.

CHARLES H. SPURGEON

Sacred Moments

We are always in the presence of God.... There is never
a non-sacred moment! His presence never diminishes.
Our awareness of His presence may falter, but the reality
of His presence never changes.

MAX LUCADO

I lie awake thinking of you,
meditating on you through the night.
Because you are my helper,
I sing for joy in the shadow of your wings.
I cling to you; your strong right hand holds me securely.

PSALM 63:6–8 NLT

The ability to see and the practice of seeing God and God's world
comes through a process of seeking and growing in intimacy with Him.

DALLAS WILLARD

Live in me. Make your home in me just as I do in you. In the same way
that a branch can't bear grapes by itself but only by being joined
to the vine, you can't bear fruit unless you are joined with me.

JOHN 15:4 MSG

Simplicity will enable you to leap lightly. Increasingly you will
find yourself living in a state of grace, finding...the sacred
in the ordinary, the mystical in the mundane.

DAVID YOUNT

Sunday, 8-20-23

> Begun and ended with encouragement; A.M. - Hebrews 6:17,18 (from _Daily Light_ and John Piper's Meditation 34 in his book _Taste and See_; P.M. - all verses from _Daily Light_ evening selection

> All other daily readings helpful as well:
- _Edges of His Ways_, Carmichael
- _Faith's checkbook_, Spurgeon ("Deliverance Not Limited")
- _Turning Points_, Jeremiah ("Trusting God; Joshua 2:24)
- _Grace for the Moment_, Vol. 1, Lucado (from his book _When God Whispers Your Name_)
- Spurgeon's _Morning and Evening_ - the evening selection
- _My Utmost for His Highest_, Chambers (continuation from Aug. 19 on Matt. 11:28 - "Come to me... I will give rest." Not "decide for," but "yield to" Christ.
- _Hope for Each Day_, Billy Graham (Isaiah 53:3 "Facing Rejection")
- _One-Minute Devotions for Women_, Larsen (Romans 1:11-12 "Sticking Together")
- _Whispers of Friendship: Daily Encouragement for Women_ ("Give It To God")

- 2 Timothy 3; Romans 1; Phil. 3+4; Prov. 20:3,15

The reflective life is a way of living that heightens
our spiritual senses to all that is sacred.

KEN GIRE

Inward Prayer

Walk and talk and work and laugh with your friends.
But behind the scenes, keep up the life of simple prayer
and inward worship. Let inward prayer be your last act
before you fall asleep and the first act when you awake.

THOMAS R. KELLY

Those who live prayerfully are constantly ready to receive
the breath of God, and to let their lives be renewed and expanded.

HENRI J. M. NOUWEN

Prayer is like love. Words pour at first. Then we are more silent and
can communicate in monosyllables. In difficulties a gesture is enough,
a word, or nothing at all—love is enough. Thus the time comes when
words are superfluous.... The soul converses with God
with a single loving glance.

CARLO CARRETTO

Enter into the inner chamber of your mind. Shut out all things
save God and whatever may aid you in seeking God;
and having barred the door of your chamber, seek Him.

ANSELM OF CANTERBURY

I ponder all your great works
and think about what you have done.
I lift my hands to you in prayer.
I thirst for you as parched land thirsts for rain.

PSALM 143:5-6 NLT

Tuesday, 8-22-23

> <u>Taste and See</u>, John Piper (ISBN 1-59052-449-7;)
Multnomah Publishers
Scripture refs. I Timothy 1:15-17 -- Meditations
44: News! News! News! Getting the Gospel and Theology
   in Right Order; pp. 135-7;
121: A Jewish Response to "The Passion of the Christ":   (The Movie produced by Mel Gibson)
   An Open Letter to Rabbi Marcia Zimmerman,
   Temple Israel; pp. 358-360;   (He sent her a copy of his book <u>The Passion of Jesus Christ</u>.)
135: The Greatest Event in History: Two Paradoxes
   in the Death of Christ; pp. 398-400.

Wed., 8-23-23

> 1 Cor. 6:13b, 18b 18c (NIV 84) — from <u>Our Daily Bread</u>
"Bible in a Year" reading

> Hymns: More Like the Master; O Love That Wilt Not
Let Me Go; Come, Ye Disconsolate; We Would See
Jesus; Still, Still With Thee; O Perfect Love, All
Human Thought Transcending (all from
<u>Worship and Service Hymnal</u>)

> "Praise God, Ye Servants of the Lord" (from <u>The Hymnbook</u>;
1912 Psalter / Wm. Bradbury) — Ps. 113

*All good meditative prayer
is a conversion of our entire self to God.*

THOMAS MERTON

Our Soul and Spirit

The very life of God, epitomized in the love of God,
originates only and always with Him.... It does not...
spring from the soil of our own souls and spirits.

W. PHILIP KELLER

God's holy beauty comes near you, like a spiritual scent,
and it stirs your drowsing soul.... He creates in you the desire to find
Him and run after Him—to follow wherever He leads you, and to press
peacefully against His heart wherever He is.

JOHN OF THE CROSS

In the very beginning it was God who formed man by His Word.
He made man in His own image. God was spirit and He gave man
a spirit so that He could come into Him and mingle
His own life with man's life.

MADAME JEANNE GUYON

The soul is a breath of living spirit, that with excellent sensitivity,
permeates the entire body to give it life. Just so, the breath of the air
makes the earth fruitful. Thus the air is the soul of the earth,
moistening it, greening it.

HILDEGARDE OF BINGEN

Friday, 8-25-23

> Hymn (verse 2) (on my mind when waking):
Before the Throne of God Above (No. 7 in
Family Songs - CC, P "publication"); author,
Charitie L. Bancroft, 1863; music, Vicki
Cook, 1997; arr. Kay Lovingood, 2007;
THRONE ROOM (8.8.8.88.8.8.8.8)

Tuesday, 8-29-23

> Voices of the Saints, Bert Ghezzi
John of Avila (No. 191; Pp. 382-3) / 1500-1569
John of God (No. 193; Pp. 386-7) / 1495-1555
Jacopone da Todi (No. 164; Pp. 328-9 / 1230?-1306
John the Baptist (No. 197; Pp. 394-5) / (First Century)

> Hymns, from The Hymnbook
327 - O Lord, My God, Most Earnestly (Ps. 63;
1912 Psalter; music: Charles Hutt Hutcheson,
1832; harmony by Geoffrey Shaw, 1925 /
STRACATHRO: C. M.) Music from Songs of
Praise, Enlarged Ed. Used by permission of
Oxford University Press. Key of A flat, with
five flats: G, A, B, D, E

*W*ho you are and what you've done are all we'll ever want.
Through the night my soul longs for you.
Deep from within me my spirit reaches out to you.

ISAIAH 26:8-9 MSG

You Are There

I look behind me and you're there,
then up ahead and you're there, too—
your reassuring presence, coming and going.
This is too much, too wonderful—
I can't take it all in!

PSALM 139:5–6 MSG.

I believe that God is in me as the sun is in the color and fragrance
of a flower—the Light in my darkness, the Voice in my silence.

HELEN KELLER

Where can I go from your Spirit?
Where can I flee from your presence?
If I go up to the heavens, you are there;
if I make my bed in the depths, you are there.
If I rise on the wings of the dawn,
if I settle on the far side of the sea,
even there your hand will guide me,
your right hand will hold me fast.

PSALM 139:7–10 NIV

Know by the light of faith that God is present,
and be content with directing all your actions toward Him.

BROTHER LAWRENCE

Tues., 8-29-23 (cont.)

> Hymns, from The Hymnbook ("Life in Christ: Pilgrimage and Guidance")
~~327~~ (previous page)

334 - Jesus, Lead the Way   Key of G, with an F sharp

Nicolaus L. von Zinzendorf, 1721

Trans. by Arthur W. Farlander, 1939

SEELENBRÄUTIGAM: 5.5.8.8.5.5

Adam Drese, 1698

Words used by permission of The Church Pension Fund.

Four verses - good for memorization, meditation, and prayer

Thurs., 8-31-23

> Hymns from The ~~Hymnal~~ Hymnbook
446 Be Known to Us in Breaking Bread (St. Flavian)
239 Come, Holy Spirit, Heavenly Dove (St. Agnes)

Tues., 9-19-23

> A.M. (wake-up) hymn! (Title?)
"Unnumbered blessings to my soul ...
O my soul, my rising soul surveys ...
from whom those blessings flow ...
I'm lost in wonder, love, and praise."

I am with you and will watch over you wherever you go.

GENESIS 28:15 NIV

Faithful Promises

Great faith isn't the ability to believe long and far into the misty future.
It's simply taking God at His word and taking the next step.

Joni Eareckson Tada

Now faith is being sure of what we hope for and certain
of what we do not see.... By faith we understand that the universe
was formed at God's command, so that what is seen was not made out
of what was visible.... And without faith it is impossible to please God,
because anyone who comes to him must believe that he exists
and that he rewards those who earnestly seek him.

Hebrews 11:1, 3, 6 niv

God takes care of His own. He knows our needs.
He anticipates our crises. He is moved by our weaknesses.
He stands ready to come to our rescue. And at just the right moment
He steps in and proves Himself as our faithful heavenly Father.

Charles Swindoll

Tuesday, Sept. 19, 2023

> John MacArthur Study Bible:

July 28, 29 (Q+A; pp. 763 & 767; Nehemiah)

Aug. 5 (Q+A, p. 791; Romans 7:7-25)

Aug. 18 (Rom. 16:1 - Phoebe; servant; Rom. 16:16 - holy

Kiss; p. 830; p. 831 - Q+A: Job's conclusion
about his debate with his friends - Job 28:23)

Wed., Sept. 20, 2023

> P.M. hymns:

"Precious Promise" (Nathaniel Niles; Philip P. Bliss)

"Never Give Up" (Fanny J. Crosby; I. Allan Sankey)

"Fade, Fade, Each Earthly Joy" (Jane C. Bonar; Theodore E. Perkins)

Thursday, Sept. 21, 2023

> P.M. hymns:

"My Redeemer" (Philip P. Bliss; James McGranahan)

"Nothing But the Blood" (Robert Lowry)

> The Gospel According to Matthew; G. Campbell
Morgan; pp. 89-94; Matthew IX: 1-17.
Healing of man brought by his friends; calling
of Matthew; God's heart as revealed to
Pharisees and John's disciples.

Let us draw near to God.... Let us hold unswervingly
to the hope we profess, for he who promised is faithful.

HEBREWS 10:22-23 NIV

His Inward Voice

Retire from the world each day to some private spot.... Stay in the secret
place till the surrounding noises begin to fade out of your heart
and a sense of God's presence envelops you.... Listen for the inward
Voice till you learn to recognize it.... Give yourself to God and then be
what and who you are without regard to what others think....
Learn to pray inwardly every moment.

A.W. TOZER

Prayer is
The world in tune,
A spirit-voice,
And vocal joys
Whose *echo* is heaven's bliss.

HENRY VAUGHN

God is not really "out there" at all. That restless heart, questioning who
you are and why you were created, that quiet voice that keeps calling
your name is not just out there, but dwells in you.

DAVID AND BARBARA SORENSEN

Come, let us worship and bow down.
Let us kneel before the LORD our maker,
for he is our God.
We are the people he watches over,
the flock under his care.
If only you would listen to his voice today!

PSALM 95:6–7 NLT

Friday, 9-22-23
> _My Utmost for His Highest_, Oswald Chambers:
   "the Missionary's Master;" John 13:13; Matt.
   23:8 (September 22nd).
> _The Gospel According to Matthew_, G. Campbell Morgan:
   Matt. XXIII:1-12; pp. 271-276.
   Friday, 9-29-23 (and days preceding)
> Memory work: from A. Carmichael's _Edges
   of His Ways_ — Sept. 20, "the thoughts of God,"
   and poem following on love; Sept. 23, Song of
   Songs 4.12,15 ("garden inclosed") — 2 stanza
   poem based on; from J. I. Packer's _Knowing
   God_; Ch. 2, "The People Who Know Their God," pp.
   31-32; 2 stanza poem (song?) about contentment;
                         (Source?)^   ^peace/
   Bert Ghezzi's _Voices of the Saints_, pp. 632-3 --
   quote from Richard Rolle (reading for Sept. 29).
> Reading / review of portions of _Mending the Soul:
   Understanding and Healing Abuse_, Steven R.
   Tracy, including footnotes. (2005, Zondervan—
   ISBN-10: 0-310-60977-1; ISBN-13: 978-0-310-
   60977-3 [both soft cover])

Joy is the echo of God's life within us.

JOSEPH MARMION

Reflections of God

Just as a prism of glass miters light and casts a colored braid,
a garden sings sweet incantations the human heart strains to hear.
Hiding in every flower, in every leaf, in every twig and bough,
are reflections of the God who once walked with us in Eden.

The heavens proclaim the glory of God.
The skies display his craftsmanship.
Day after day they continue to speak;
night after night they make him known.
They speak without a sound or word;
their voice is never heard.
Yet their message has gone throughout the earth,
and their words to all the world.

PSALM 19:1–4 NLT

Woven in a perfect way, a blanket of stars covers the night sky,
each star set in its place, reflecting its perfect light. All the stars together
make a grand display, glimmering and shimmering
in a unique expression of praise to the Creator of them all.

WENDY MOORE

I see nature...playing endless variations in design and beauty....
In such simple yet eloquent ways, I am reminded that God is personal,
revealing Himself continuously in the finite.

JUDITH LECHMAN

Wed., 10-04-23

> Hymns: from <u>Praise and Worship Hymnal</u>
(Kansas City, MO: Lillenas Publishing Co.) –
210, "A Touch of New Fire," Mrs. C.H. Morris;
from <u>Crowning Glory Hymnal</u> (Grand Rapids, Mich.:
Zondervan Publishing House) – 370, "Give Me
thy Heart," Eliza E. Hewitt / William J. Kirkpatrick;
369, "Ring the Bells of Heaven," William O. Cushing /
George F. Root; 368, "You May Have the Joy-Bells,"
J. Edw. Ruark / William J. Kirkpatrick

Thursday, 10-05-23

> Re: 1 Cor. 15:29 – could there be any
correspondence with 1 Cor. 7:12-16?
~~The~~ <u>Eerdman's' Handbook to the Bible</u>[*] gives
two possibilities: either people (believers) being
baptized on behalf of unbelievers or being
baptized in recognition of believing friends
or relatives who preceded them in death, as
a way of acknowledging the hope of being
reunited with them.
[*] ISBN 0-8028-3436-1 (Alexander, David, 1937-?;
                                    pictures)

The tiniest dewdrop hanging from a grass blade in the morning
is big enough to reflect the sunshine and the blue of the sky.

Guideposts

To be glad of life, because it gives you the chance to love
and to work and to play and to look up at the stars; to be satisfied
with your possessions, but not contented with yourself until you have
made the best of them;...to think seldom of your enemies,
often of your friends, and every day of Christ; and to spend
as much time as you can, with body and with spirit
in God's out-of-doors—these are little guideposts
on the footpath to peace.

HENRY VAN DYKE

We do not understand the intricate pattern of the stars in their courses,
but we know that He who created them does, and that just as surely as
He guides them, He is charting a safe course for us.

BILLY GRAHAM

A new path lies before us;
We're not sure where it leads;
But God goes on before us,
Providing all our needs.
This path, so new, so different
Exciting as we climb,
Will guide us in His perfect will
Until the end of time.

LINDA MAURICE

Friday, 10-06-23

> MacArthur Study Bible (NKJV) - Sept. 1-4 notes
on Song of Solomon (theme etc.) and 1 Cor.
12-14 (spiritual gifts; love/marriage). See
p. 844 comparison of Song of Sol. 8:6,7
with 1 Cor. 13:1-8.

> Days of Praise (ICR) - Oct. 6, 2006: Helpful
exposition of Matt. 20:8, "Working By Faith,"
Henry M. Morris, Ph.D. Early laborers sought
contract agreement unlike later laborers who
trusted "the lord of the vineyard" as "a man of
integrity and justice." Makes comparison with
heavenly rewards, referencing "opportunities, motivation, and
trust in the Lord."

> Tabletalk (Ligonier) - Oct. 2016, the 16th Century:
p. 28, "How Vocation Transformed Society," by
Gene Edward Veith of Fort Wayne, Indiana
(emeritus lit. prof., provost, Patrick Henry College;
dir., Cranach Inst. @ Concordia Theological Seminary)

The signposts of GOD are clear and point out the right road.
The life-maps of GOD are right, showing the way to joy.

PSALM 19:7–8 MSG

Friendship with God

O the pure delight of a single hour
that before Thy throne I spend,
When I kneel in prayer, and with Thee, my God,
I commune as friend with friend!

FANNY J. CROSBY

Friendship with God is a two-way street.... Jesus said that He tells
His friends all that His Father has told Him; close friends communicate
thoroughly and make a transfer of heart and thought. How awesome
is our opportunity to be friends with God, the almighty Creator of all!

BEVERLY LAHAYE

God-friendship is for God-worshipers;
They are the ones he confides in.

PSALM 25:14 MSG

Meditation is the activity of calling to mind, and thinking over,
and dwelling on, and applying to oneself, the various things that one
knows about the works and ways and purposes and promises of God.
It is an activity of holy thought, consciously performed
in the presence of God, under the eye of God, by the help of God,
as a means of communion with God.

J. I. PACKER

Sunday, Oct. 29, 2023
> <u>My Utmost for His Highest</u>, Oswald Chambers –
"Substitution," 2 Cor. 5:21. "It is not Christ
for me unless I am determined to have Christ
formed in me."
> Hymns: (in <u>Worship and Service Hymnal</u>)
257, "He Lives" (Alfred H. Ackley, words & music)
358, "I Would Be Like Jesus" (James Rowe,
   words; Bentley D. Ackley, music)
Both copyrighted by The Rodeheaver Co. –
257 in 1933; 358 in 1912, renewed 1940
Tuesday, 10-31-2023
> ICR's <u>Days of Praise</u>, Sept.-Oct.-Nov.
2006; "The Mystery of Darkness," by Henry
M. Morris, Ph.D., Tuesday, October 31.
Based on Revelation 22:5; additional
references: 1 John 1:5; Rev. 21:25 (c̄
Rev. 22:5); Isaiah 45:6-7; Eph. 6:12;
John 3:19; Romans 13:12; Jude 13;
1 Peter 2:9; Col. 1:13; Eph. 5:11.

$\mathcal{G}$od's friendship is the unexpected joy we find
when we reach for His outstretched hand.

JANET L. WEAVER SMITH

New Life of Love

So, chosen by God for this new life of love, dress in the wardrobe God
picked out for you: compassion, kindness, humility, quiet strength,
discipline. Be even-tempered, content with second place,
quick to forgive an offense. Forgive as quickly and completely as the
Master forgave you. And regardless of what else you put on, wear love.
It's your basic, all-purpose garment. Never be without it.

COLOSSIANS 3:12–14 MSG

Look deep within yourself and recognize what brings life
and grace into your heart. It is this that can be shared
with those around you. You are loved by God.
This is an inspiration to love.

CHRISTOPHER DE VINCK

When God's power touches a mere human being, something happens!
Creation all over again! The life-changing touch of love!

GLORIA GAITHER

Faith in God gives your life a center from which you can
reach out and dare to love the world.

BARBARA FARMER

Tuesday, 10-31-2023

> Ligonier's _Tabletalk Magazine_, October 2017:
Daily Bible Studies: Into The Word, October 31.
Based on R.C. Sproul's teaching series,
"Preachers and Preaching." Scripture Refs.
included for "Our Highest Calling" are
Isa. 52:7 (chief ref.); 1 Pet. 2:9;
Matt. 28:18-20; Nahum 1:15; Rom. 10:14-15;
Eph. 3:7-13; 1 Tim. 5:17.

> Oswald Chambers' _My Utmost for His Highest_ –
"The Discernment of Faith," Matt. 17:20
(October 31st).

✱ Sat., Nov. 18, 2023   (Chambers' read Sun., 11-19-23)
> Oswald Chambers, _My Utmost for His Highest_ –
"Winning Into Freedom," John 8:36 ..."personality,"
"I can't," "tyranny of individuality"; Gal. 2:20

> Andrew Murray, _Abide in Christ: The Joy of
Being in God's Presence_; Ch. 8 – As Your
Righteousness, p.67. I Cor. 1:30 RV; Ps. 45:7.
Whitaker House (1 John 2:28) – New Kensington, PA;
ISBN-13: 978-0-88368-860-1; ISBN-10: 0-88368-860-3

_L_ove others for the sake of God.
Love God for His own sake.

AUGUSTINE

Gift of the Ordinary

We encounter God in the ordinariness of life, not in the search
for spiritual highs and extraordinary, mystical experiences,
but in our simple presence in life.

BRENNAN MANNING

May our lives be illumined
by the steady radiance
renewed daily,
of a wonder,
the source of which
is beyond reason.

DAG HAMMARSKJÖLD

Why is everyone hungry for more?... ✓
I have God's more-than-enough,
More joy in one ordinary day
Than they get in all their shopping sprees.
At day's end I'm ready for sound sleep,
For you, God, have put my life back together.

PSALM 4:6–8 MSG

The sun...in its full glory, either at rising or setting—
this, and many other like blessings we enjoy daily;
and for the most of them, because they are so common,
most men forget to pay their praises. But let not us.

IZAAK WALTON

Sun., 11-19-23

> Recent hymns from <u>Worship & Service Hymnal</u>:

447 - "O Lord of Heaven and Earth and Sea;"
      Christopher Wordsworth / Charles F. Gounod
         (19th century); Radiant Morn (8, 8, 8, 4)

442 - "Father, Whose Will Is Life and Good;"
      Hardwicke D. Rawnsley (d. 1920) / Thomas
      Tallis (16th century); Tallis' Ordinal - C.M.
         (8, 6, 8, 6)

37 - "There's a Song in the Air;" Josiah G. Holland,
1819 - 1881 / Karl P. Harrington, 1861 - 1953;
Christmas Song (6, 6, 6, 6, 12, 12)

Find e.e. cummings quote to high school student
about self-love (mentioned on Guidelines program
by Harold Sala - BBN Radio, 12-11-2019.
Scripture ref. Rom. 12:3 - Sala believes there's
a difference between self-love and loving self.

Walking with God

My Lord God, I have no idea where I am going.
I do not see the road ahead of me. I cannot know for certain
where it will end.... But I believe that the desire to please You
does in fact please You. And I hope I have that desire
in all that I am doing. I hope that I will never do anything apart
from that desire. And I know that if I do this, You will lead me
by the right road though I may know nothing about it.

Therefore will I trust You always, though I may seem to be lost
and in the shadow of death. I will not fear, for You are ever with me.
And You will never leave me to face my perils alone.

THOMAS MERTON

God gets down on His knees among us; gets on our level
and shares Himself with us. He does not reside afar off
and send diplomatic messages, He kneels among us....
God shares Himself generously and graciously.

EUGENE PETERSON

Sunday, Dec. 3, 2023

> Luke 1:1-17; Matt. 1:18-21
> early A.M. hymns: "Silent Night"; "Come, ye Thankful
  People, Come"; "We've a Story to Tell to the Nations"
> Moody's Today in the Word, Dec. 2007: The Image of
  God as Parent. Inside cover — "Today with Pres.
  Easley," Luke 11:11-13; 1 John 3; "Theology Matters,"
  by John Koessler (.com) — God's naming himself
  father; Malachi 1:6 — not like Shakespeare's
  "a rose by any other name . . . ". More available
  in Koessler's Moody Press book, God Our Father.
> ICR's Days of Praise: Jan. 2010 — Jan. 18,
  "Prayer and Supplication," Phil. 4:6 et al.; HMM III
  "The Father of All," Malachi 2:10; 1:11; HMM (Jan. 23)
> Hymn: "When Morning Gilds the Skies" (19th cent.,
  translated from the German)
> ICR's Days of Praise, Dec. 3, 2009: "The Rainbow
  and the Cloud," Rev. 10:1; 1:7, 13-16; 10:2; 21:1;
  Gen. 2:5; 1:7; 9:13; Eph. 3:21; HMM

*Yet I am always with you;
you hold me by my right hand.*

PSALM 73:23 NIV

Breath of the Soul

As prayer moves into the subconscious mind, breathed longings
of wonder and adoration seem always underneath
and in the background of everything—a little like a tune that we
suddenly realize we have been humming all day long.

RICHARD J. FOSTER

God says to His children: Are you lonesome? Breathe out My name.
Come to Me and I will be your friend. Are you sick? Come to Me
for healing. Are you left out of things? Feeling rejected
and pushed aside? Come home to Me.

ALICE CHAPIN

So faith bounds forward to its goal in God,
and love can trust her Lord to lead her there;
upheld by Him my soul is following hard,
till God hath full fulfilled my deepest prayer.

FREDERICK BROOK

I love the LORD because he hears my voice
and my prayer for mercy.
Because he bends down to listen,
I will pray as long as I have breath!

PSALM 116:1–2 NLT

Wed., 12-20-23
> Pss. 22; 23; 24   (ESV)
  Ps. 22: 15a; 19; 21b; 27-28
  Malachi 1:14b; cross-refs.: Ps. 47:2; 76:12 (v.v. 11,12)
  Friday, 12-22-23
> Hymn: God Our Refuge and Our Strength
> Prayer poems: Richard Rolle (B. Ghezzi);
  A. Carmichael's Edges of His Ways;
  Sept. 20th: Brave Love; hope; faith;
  sum of life, love
> Hymns: O Love That Will Not Let Me Go;
  Lead Me to Calvary

Prayer is the breath of the soul.
OLE HALLESBY

Contemplating God

We are so preciously loved by God that we cannot
even comprehend it. No created being can ever know how much
and how sweetly and tenderly God loves them. It is only with the help
of His grace that we are able to persevere in spiritual contemplation
with endless wonder at His high, surpassing, immeasurable love
which our Lord in His goodness has for us.

JULIAN OF NORWICH

Take a moment to consider the awesome reality that the God
who spoke and created the universe is now speaking to you. If Jesus
could speak and raise the dead, calm a storm...and heal the incurable,
then what effect might a word from Him have upon your life?

HENRY T. BLACKABY

When I look at the night sky and see the work of your fingers—
the moon and the stars you set in place—
what are mere mortals that you should think about them,
human beings that you should care for them?

PSALM 8:3–4 NLT

Sunday, Jan. 21, 2024
> early A.M. hymns: This Is the Day; How
  Long Has It Been
> John 16:26; no need for intermediaries -- prayer
  made directly to the Father
WED. - Jan. 31, 2024
> Voices of the Saints, B. Ghezzi:
  John Bosco; Monica; Marcella
Other readings:
  • Whispers of Friendship - Albert
    Schweitzer, "Rekindle the Inner Spirit"
  • Faith's Checkbook, C.H. Spurgeon,
    "God Always Hears" (Micah 7:7)
  • Grace for the Moment, M. Lucado,
    "The Lord Is Peace," Phil. 4:7;
    Judges 6:24 (Gideon)
  • Leben (periodical: Jul-Sep 2007;
    Vol. 3, Issue 3): George Washington
    Carver article by Kate Uttinger with
    photos. Carver hired by ~~Booket~~ Booker
    T. Washington to teach @ Tuskegee.

Contemplation is nothing else but a secret, peaceful,
and loving infusion of God, which, if admitted,
will set the soul on fire with the spirit of love.

JOHN OF THE CROSS

Nature's Retreat

The deep woods reveal God's presence. The way the golden sunlight
streaks through the lush greens and browns of a summer wood
is nothing short of divine. In the fall the profusion of colors
makes every leaf a prayer. Winter's snow transforms the woods
into a cathedral. Even the dark, drab hues of the woods
in early spring speak of hope and resurrection. It is a place
where I can be on a spiritual retreat.

RAYMOND K. PETRUCCI

I love to think of nature as an unlimited broadcasting station through
which God speaks to us every hour, if only we will tune in.

GEORGE WASHINGTON CARVER

If we are children of God, we have a tremendous treasure in nature
and will realize that it is holy and sacred. We will see God reaching out
to us in every wind that blows, every sunrise and sunset, every cloud
in the sky, every flower that blooms, and every leaf that fades.

OSWALD CHAMBERS

For great is your love, reaching to the heavens;
your faithfulness reaches to the skies.
Be exalted, O God, above the heavens;
let your glory be over all the earth.

PSALM 57:10–11 NIV

WED., Jan. 31, 2024 (Cont.)

> Readings:

- <u>Turning Points</u> (2005 devotional book by David Jeremiah); Jan. 25 - "A Lesson in Humility;" Prov. 11:2; example from Booker T. Washington's life re: his servant attitude & friendliness

- <u>Hope for Each Day</u>, Billy Graham; January 31: "Godly Thoughts"; Rom. 12:2

- <u>My Utmost for His Highest</u>, Oswald Chambers; January 31st: "Do You See Your Calling?"; Rom. 1:1; 9:3

- <u>Forward Day by Day</u>, Nov./Dec. 2010/Jan. 2011 — MONDAY, January 31; Psalm 57:7; Topic: fixing one's attention on Jesus.... conversion equals entire and intense interest in him.

- <u>Days of Praise</u>, Dec. '09/Jan.-Feb. '10 — Sunday, January 31; Isa. 45:18; Gen. 1:1, 2; "formed to Be Inhabited;" Gap theory debunked.

Step by Step

Our Heavenly Father...wants us to reach up and take His hand,
but He doesn't want us to *ever* let go. In fact, His desire is that we
become *more* and *more* dependent upon Him for every step.
That's because He wants to take us to places we've never been.
To heights we can't even imagine.... God always requires the first step
to be ours. In order to take that first step, we must look into
the face of God, reach up and take His hand,
and say, "Lead me in the path You have for me, Lord.
From this day on I want to walk with You."

STORMIE OMARTIAN

Whoso draws nigh to God
One step through doubtings dim,
God will advance a mile
In blazing light to him.

Your walk with God is essential. His heart is not seen
in an occasional chat or weekly visit. We learn His will
as we take up residence in His house every single day.

MAX LUCADO

For we walk by faith, not by sight.

2 CORINTHIANS 5:7 NKJV

Tues., 01-30-24

> Readings re: job loss - Billy Graham's _Hope for
Each Day_ - "Living Stones;" 1 Peter 2:5.
See also RBC Ministries Discovery Series
booklet, "_Now What? The Healing Journey
Through Job Loss_, by Chuck Fridsma (RBC
employee); © 2009 RBC Ministries, Grand
Rapids, Michigan.

> _Tabletalk Mag._, June 2017, lead articles : "Blessed Are:
• the Meek," by Ken Jones (Glendale Mssy. Bap. Ch.,
Miami, FL)
• the Merciful," by Gary Steward (Colorado Chr. U.; author,
Princeton Seminary)
(1812 - 1929)

> _Tabletalk Mag._, January 2018 - Wednesday, Jan.
31 : Jesus The Savior; Acts 13:23. Examples -
military rescue; physical healing; spiritual
separation from God (sin), the most important of
all. Other scripture refs. : Matt. 1:21; Rev. 21;
Ps. 17:7; Isa. 49:26; Titus 2:11-14; 1 Jn. 4:14.

_The Lord's goodness surrounds us at every moment. I walk through it
almost with difficulty, as through thick grass and flowers._

R. W. BARBER

God's Living Word

For the word of God is living and active and sharper
than any two-edged sword, and piercing as far as the division of soul
and spirit, of both joints and marrow, and able to judge the thoughts
and intentions of the heart. And there is no creature hidden
from His sight, but all things are open and laid bare to the eyes
of Him with whom we have to do.

HEBREWS 4:12–13 NASB

With my whole heart have I sought You;
Oh, let me not wander from Your commandments!
Your word I have hidden in my heart,
that I might not sin against You.

PSALM 119:10–11 NKJV

Every part of Scripture is God-breathed and useful
one way or another—showing us truth, exposing our rebellion,
correcting our mistakes, training us to live God's way.
Through the Word we are put together
and shaped up for the tasks God has for us.

2 TIMOTHY 3:16–17 MSG

Friday, Feb 9, 2024

A Daily Journey through Psalms, Day 39 —

"Beyond the Status Quo" (Eph. 4:23-24):

You are being renewed in the spirit of your [HCSB] minds; you put on the new man, the one created according to God's likeness in the righteousness and purity of the truth.

Also Ps. 145:10 (NASB):

All your works shall give thanks to You, O LORD, And your godly ones shall bless You.

On not being in a rut — "no place for disciples who are dejected, discouraged, or disheartened." Make necessary changes — seek God's better plan. Changes "your heart tells you are right." (Uh, oh—not per Jon Bloom of Desiring God Ministries)

Franklin Graham quote also cited — "There is not a single thing that Jesus cannot change, control, and conquer because He is the living Lord."

When we give the Word of God space to live in our heart, the Spirit of God will use it to take root, penetrating the earthiest recesses of our lives.

KEN GIRE

Joy in His Presence

We must drink deeply from the very Source the deep calm
and peace of interior quietude and refreshment of God,
allowing the pure water of divine grace to flow plentifully
and unceasingly from the Source itself.

MOTHER TERESA

When God finds a soul that rests in Him and is not easily moved,
He operates within it in His own manner. That soul allows God to do
great things within it. He gives to such a soul the key to the treasures
He has prepared for it so that it might enjoy them. And to this same
soul He gives the joy of His presence which entirely absorbs such a soul.

CATHERINE OF GENOA

What extraordinary delight we find in the presence of God.
He draws us in, His welcome so fresh and inviting.

As we keep his commands, we live deeply and surely in him,
and he lives in us. And this is how we experience his deep
and abiding presence in us: by the Spirit he gave us.

1 JOHN 3:24 MSG

Sunday, ~~July~~ August 13, 2023
> Psalm 33 – *Our Daily Bread's* "Forever Faithful God," by
Xochitl Dixon (vv. 1-11); Mike Ross's *The Light of the Psalms*,
Day 101 : Blessed Is the Nation, pp. 180-1.
>   1 John 4:7-5:12 ; Acts 15:13-18 (see also
Amos 9:11-12, and *Bible Knowledge Commentary-*
N.T., pp. 394-5, which includes millennial
interpretations discussion). Also see BKT-N.T.
1 John 5:6 discussion for "false teachers" info.
> Hymn : "Lord, For Tomorrow and Its Needs" (words written by
Sybil F. Partridge (pseudonym for Sister Mary
Xavier)
Friday, Feb. 9, 2024
> *Hope for Each Day*, Billy Graham
February 9 : Power to Change the World;
Ps. 71:5 – You are my hope, O Lord God;
You are my trust from my youth.
On loving and serving God because of
"the Cross" and the hope it provides.

A quiet morning with a loving God puts the events
of the upcoming day into proper perspective.

JANETTE OKE

Ellie Claire™ Gift & Paper Corp.
Minneapolis, MN 55438
www.ellieclaire.com

Be Still and Know that I Am God
Promise Journal
© 2010 by Ellie Claire™ Gift & Paper Corp.

ISBN 978-1-60936-009-2

Compiled by Barbara Farmer
Cover and interior design by Lisa and Jeff Franke

Printed in China.